College Survival Guide

you are not alone

Paula Laureen Henderson, BA

Gumdrop Enterprise
Saskatoon, Saskatchewan, Canada

Published and distributed with the authorization of:
Gumdrop Enterprise
Saskatoon, Saskatchewan, Canada

College Survival Guide: You Are Not Alone

First Edition published electronically in Canada, 2006

First Edition paperback printed in Canada, 2007

Full-color e-book sold exclusively at: **www.knowledgevault.ca**

Book design: Dezyne Aide by Lisa, Saskatoon, Saskatchewan

Candy machine image: Karl Rogalsky, Saskatoon, Saskatchewan

Eiffel Tower photo: Nita Carvalho, Windsor, Ontario

Copyeditors:
Donald M. Henderson
Mary E. H. Hilger
Stefanie Hutchinson

Our team is dedicated to excellence and we have made every effort for accuracy. We genuinely apologize for any minor errors that may have occurred with the quotes. For further clarification or necessary changes, contact Gumdrop Enterprise: gumdropenterprise@hotmail.com

ISBN 978-0-9783141-0-1

Printed by Houghton Boston
in Saskatoon, Saskatchewan, Canada

Dedicated to Emilia Mudryk,
my grandmother and author
who taught me to fly.
She would be so proud of who
her grandchildren are becoming.

Acknowledgements

I would like to thank you Jesus, for teaching me to dream. You are worthy to serve, and you have never failed me.

Father, you pushed me this summer to become a better writer, and you are right; status quo is not good enough for me. Dad, thank you for being bold enough to tell your daughter to risk it all.

Mother, you taught me how to laugh with your delightful late night stories. After a lifetime of watching you pray, I am thoroughly convinced that Jesus is real.

Lisa Rogalsky: You are my friend, on-demand designer (often against your will), breakout partner, cheerleader, chicken soup fetcher, world's best pumpkin soup maker, distraction creator, wisdom giver, censorship authority, iron sharpener, favourite comfort food sharer, and most of all a Godly woman who believes all things are possible through Christ who strengthens us!

Mary E. H. Hilger: Without you, the book would not be finished! I am so proud of who you have become, and how patient you have learned to be. You really are a profound teacher, and inspired me to reach for excellence. Your steadiness has always filled me with admiration.

Nita Carvalho: For telling me to stop thinking sooo much. You just want me to be me. Your admirable work ethic even makes me want to do the dishes on occasion. P.S. Thank you, my best and dear friend, for letting me share the "chocolate chip cookie story".

Shelley Liu: Thank you for telling me to get out of my pajamas and keep writing.

Table of Contents

CHAPTER ONE   9
College did not teach us to dream
Dare to Dream!

CHAPTER TWO   31
College did not teach us how to balance
a checkbook
No Money, Honey?

CHAPTER THREE   53
College did not teach us how to be social
Care to Connect

CHAPTER FOUR   75
College did not teach us to learn
No Pain, No Brain!

CHAPTER FIVE   103
College did not teach us about
cyber world
"Wired and Global"

CHAPTER SIX   123
College did not teach us how to listen
Ears to Hear

CHAPTER SEVEN   145
College did not protect our ethics
**G-Vegas: what goes on
here, stays here!**

CHAPTER EIGHT   169
College did not teach us how to be
global citizens
"College is just a tool"

CHAPTER ONE

College did not teach us to dream

Dare to Dream!

As I slowly sipped my stale, truck-stop coffee with powdered creamer still floating in clumps at the top of my cup, I rolled my grubby menthol cigarette with my fingers and watched the smoky mist filtrate the air. The musty smell and swirls of smoke were teasing my easy going, yet thrill-seeking, high school classmates who were sitting at the table with me. I was a seventeen year old artist who wore all black religiously, was still angry with my parents for divorcing when I was young, and attended a high school with subversive artistic rebels who were capable of crashing the town computer mainframe with the ugliest of viruses. My closest friends, who grew up in my dysfunctional world with me, knew that I wanted to do something with my life and travel somewhere exciting. I was willing to go anywhere at least an hour away from my small, dusty western prairie town, and they were often confused by my disenchantment. The United States of America was in the middle of the 'Gulf War' and I was hesitant to even make any college plans, in the event that my nation of Canada might not even exist by the time I was to go to college!

I remember hearing the words which were often chanted by my family, *"You have a destiny,"* ring in my ears. "Your dreams are too big for here," my mother always whispered to me on the phone whenever I called her frantically at work, because I needed the car we were sharing. I thought to myself that her encouraging words about my potential and destiny were just what doting mothers always say to their kids, to get them to stop stewing about life and be happy with their first fast-food job. I thought that was just her and other family members trying to push me towards college, manipulating me to bring up my marks in my senior year. I knew that as a teenager I had big dreams— I just didn't know how to chase my dreams from where I was living. I looked around at all of my co-workers wearing orange and navy polyester, squirting each other with ketchup—and saw myself being slowly sucked into the dark vortex of minimum wage earners for an eternity.

It seemed to me that everyone would start talking about my future when I was a junior in high school, but they never offered me any solid answers! It was as if they wanted to control my destiny that I hadn't even discovered yet. I didn't even know that I had a destiny in grade 11. All of those adult expectations just made my senior year even more stressful. Worst of all, there was no defense even if I had objections to family pressure. Even if I had a dream...

How do I get from here to there, I thought?
What am I to do with me?!

One year later, however, I was energized in my senior year of high school because the Gulf War was over thirty seconds after it began; I had a new zippy little grey hatchback car that enabled me to eat at a new funky truck stop in the next town 30 miles from mine; and I was beginning to realize that I was headed for college. I was smart enough to realize that it was a perfect escape route from living with my parents, who were way too concerned about my fuel costs and the friends I ate pizza with. I was dreaming about the same thing that millions of high school students dream of.

One day I was going to attend college, where I would not ever have to hear myself say, "Yes, father, that is not where my coat and school bag belong..." as he pointed at my school books and clothes scattered all over the living room, kitchen and bathroom. I thought that once I had my posh high-rise downtown apartment in the city—with a spacious balcony large enough for the barbecue and patio furniture I would be able to afford—I would have *FREEDOM, FREEDOM, and more FREEDOM, baby!* Every afternoon after class I would get to wear my plaid, funky boxer shorts and a hopelessly sexy, black tank top, while sitting on the hardwood floor of my apartment eating pop tarts and peanut butter off of my own knife that I was free to lick.

Never again would I have to hear my mother say 'vegetables are appropriate with all three meals'. Who was going to cook meals? Heck, once I made it to college I was going to live off of chicken wings, pizza and chocolate milkshakes five nights a week!!! I would never again have to scheme how I was going to throw a party while my father and stepmother were vacationing in Scotland—I could have one in my own upscale apartment, with lots of unhealthy food and "free" alcoholic drinks. I dreamt about what every intelligent girl dreams about in high school. I was going to escape my home town where everyone knew me all too well—and my parents were actually going to help me pay for it!!

I remember in my senior year of high school checking the mail every day for an acceptance letter. One morning, after routinely harassing the fragile mailman who was tired of my demands, I saw with nervous delight that my envelope had arrived. My hands were shaking as I opened the crisp white letter postmarked from the college I wished desperately to attend (let's be honest—anyone that would let me in). I dreamed of not only excelling scholastically, but I wanted to cheer on the good-looking football team when they played, and I dreamed of attending funky cafés with my classmates.

As I unfolded the letter and looked at the formal college insignia, my knees began to tremble. I searched earnestly for a cheerful sentence proclaiming wonderful news. I found it—I was accepted! Thank God!!! I was getting far, far away from the small prairie town that I thought was suffocating my soul, because I was too young to understand what my community would one day mean to me. To this day, I have not experienced that same kind of thrill and exhilaration. All hopes and dreams appear finalized in one acceptance letter. It is the one sentence that convinces all parents to not only *help* their child leave, but also help their child *pay* for that departure.

It is done, I thought; *now I just have to get there!* I was convinced that the only task I needed to accomplish that summer before attending my first year was to convince my parents, who had already been supporting my older brothers and older sister in college, that I could register for classes myself. They did not need to travel to the college with me to inspect the condition of my sleeping quarters! I was convinced that I would be bolder than my sister was during her first year, as I left home to champion all of the youthful reasons for independence. Truthfully, I recall drawing blood in my mother's arm, because I was clasping her too tightly as we entered the monstrous metropolis of post-secondary education.

Not only did I have a knot in my stomach for two weeks, but I had to daily resist the urge to call home in tears, so my parents could reassure me that they hadn't turned my bedroom into their new office. As I sat in my dusty, cold basement suite, I suddenly began to replay all of the sweet, sensitive, soothing words whispered by my mother. Oddly, once you've paid your first month's rent, her advice does not feel like nagging—even if you are too young to admit it yet.

My mother, who had already "done" the college experience more than once, was no longer overly exaggerating as "queen of the henpeckers". When she said I would face cultural adjustments going from western Canada to studying in the east, her truthful advice suddenly became a voice of caring reason.

I just assumed in my youthful ignorance that college was simply a harder version of high school, where teachers are there to help you and explain things twice. I assumed that all administrators were paid to be in their office any time of the day to receive my call, to answer my questions because I didn't look through my college handbook. I just assumed that because I was wearing the coolest pair of jeans in the whole room, surely they would remember my name and want to come running out of their office to serve me whenever I needed scholastic assistance. I thought that an advisor would phone me at home and not only make sure I had registered for the right classes, but have my books ready at their office for me.

I thought as a young teenager that the college was going to help me with all the details and that my summer would only be spent looking for a tight, posh apartment to live in, while planning my wardrobe for each of my classes. I was a diva; the root of all life experiences evolved around my shi-shi (chic) wardrobe! Oh, if only that was the way that the college system and life works. College and university are not only difficult scholastically; attending classes is a full time career, demanding hard work. Youthful visions blind realistic perceptions of university, because young students have not actually had the glorious experience of filing taxes yet. Once they file taxes for the first time, there's an eerie realization of *why* they need the income they are dreaming about. By the second month of paying rent for the miserable basement suite that I could barely afford, I soon realized why I was trying to receive my degree!

As I walked down the street with my new frightened roommate to the local fast food hangout (because we couldn't afford the trendy cappuccino bar),

I thought longingly of the day we would be able to afford a hot steaming latté. I didn't realize in my freshman year that the only reason funky students dressed in black are sitting in the downtown café is to stare longingly at the high school students who *can* afford a muffin with their coffee. The college artisans are waiting to use the public phone while they watch high school students remind them of "the good ol' days". They have just one hour to find the apartment that their buddy "skidder" suggested, after waiting in line for two hours trying to buy leftover math textbooks.

The funky students are only using the public phone because they have lost their phone line…uhhh…again. Even though they have only been attending college for two weeks, they're looking for an apartment because they've learned what ZERO TOLERANCE means, and have been kicked out of the dorms for using drugs. Now that they are sober and cannot afford "homemade brownies", they understand *why* that $1000 non-refundable deposit was really worth obeying the rules.

Although I am thankful for all the advice my mentors gave me, I spent my freshman and sophomore years wishing that an experienced college veteran or alumni had sat down with me to give some helpful tips. (For example… how to keep my phone from being disconnected—give or take a couple of times). I would also have loved to learn before trying to vacuum my laptop computer (to avoid buying the expensive wipes) that the suction from the vacuum cleaner will rip the keys right off the keyboard! Let me assure you, you'll lose a lot of time digging through the vacuum cleaner bag looking for your #9 and #0 keys, while thinking of a better-sounding story to tell the computer service advisor that is handling your "special case".

While university is a very defining season of your life, it is only four to six years of your life. I have graduated now and have embarked on a new and equally thrilling part of my life. However, I have experienced some heartbreaking lessons while attending classes. Helping just one freshman and their parents avoid the pitfalls that I fell into will assure me that words of wisdom rescue the lost.

After my best friend and I graduated in the east from Bible school, we decided over the summer to pursue a degree—applying to the same university in the United States. We both 'scrambled' that summer to earn enough money to survive in Virginia—if we were lucky enough to get accepted. By the month of August we were both accepted into our first school of choice, and we were ecstatic! Unfortunately, our best fundraising efforts were not enough to attend in September; we had to postpone class enrolment while we pursued scholarships, finally arriving in January.

My former roommate and I had only travelled to the United States on vacation, and I had never personally been to the south—so attending university in Virginia was quite an adventure for me. Over the phone, we began planning how we were going to decorate our dorm rooms, which events we were going to attend, and agreed to sign up for the same classes together. As best friends, we were united in our philosophical views and inherently agreed that an early morning statistics class was unacceptable.

That is what freshmen in university do; they schedule classes together, rather than discovering what best suits their program. They do this because they think it will be fun to be in class together, giving each other confidence while attending a frightening new university. They don't realize that they will spend the entire class time glaring at their best friend for using up their incredibly expensive shampoo. They will think of diabolical ways to torture them—like phoning the university accounting department and telling them that your roommate's parents would love to make an extra tuition payment by that Friday. Or in my case, like going through my roommate's favorite Oreo cookies and eating all the icing filling in the middle, putting the leftover cookie shells back together, and tucking them neatly back into the cookie bag. Psychologists and cartoon characters call my personality type *subversive!*

We were so excited before we had packed the car and headed south. We assumed that an American university would be caring; the 'little glitches' in international paperwork would be solved when we arrived. My best friend and I did not comprehend that when we drove from Canada to Virginia without valid student visas and bank statements ready at the border, we *would* be detained. **International students:** be forewarned that you must be able to prove your financial ability, in a lengthy document, to reside in the country without incurring expense to the American people.

Sitting in a musty border patrol office, we sat on very uncomfortable hardwood chairs, designed especially to punish lippy teenagers. I discovered that they will keep you a few hours longer if you are a smart alley cat like me, foolishly asking the border official if he knows Saddam Hussein personally. Border patrol officers will not feel sorry for young adults who have not eaten all day while they wait for clarification from immigration officials. We frantically faxed family members for verification of finances.

Survival Tip #1:

Do not vex local police or any administrators who are capable of failing you, suing you, and/or arresting you. Leave that for when you phone home to tell your father that you can't afford the rent for October.

It was during that long painful wait, as I retired from arguing with border patrol men, that I began to ask myself... *why am I going to university in the United States of America?* Most students would naturally ask that before getting lippy with an angry American man dressed in blue; however, some of us youthfully like to jump, and then look. If you are jumping off a steep cliff without a bungee cord, there is a shockingly slight chance that you are going to get hurt or lose your life.

As we drove to the university together, we took our time to experience American life while we traveled. Yes, we planned to show up the night before registration; that way we wouldn't get nervous while learning the city landscapes, roads, nearest police stations, or grocery stores that would be open past 10 p.m. We did not get there too early, so as to avoid placing a burden upon ourselves regarding which bank we would use, which gym we would work out in, and which church we would attend. We were young, life was thrilling, and those decisions were just boring details! Unfortunately, when you are traveling away from home—even if it is only 50 miles away— the details are important. Especially when you are eating a stale chocolate bar at a gas station in Pennsylvania, while the suspicious locals watch you study a road map dated 1957, because that is all they have left.

Sitting in the 10,000-seat auditorium to register for classes, we became acutely aware of being in a system much bigger than we'd ever known. That auditorium alone was six times the size of my small town. As we sat there waiting for immunization, we longingly dreamt of the summer before arriving at university. We could remember the cheers, weeping with those who had helped us get there; and until we left, the parties were unending. We both chose to stay and endure the hardships, because we felt guilty by how estatic our families were for us, running straight to the phone to call close family members. Parents love using guilt (the gift that keeps on giving) to make sure that you endure the entire year without quitting. It is their way of saying, *"If you fail, costing us even more money that we do not have, we will hunt you down like a dog and make you flip burgers for a year to pay us back!".*

Long before you pack your one suitcase with all that you think you will need, ask yourself one very important question:

"What is my passion?"

Your passion is *what* you are doing and *why* you are here. Your passion, or your dreams as some would call it, is part of your destiny designed by God. An indicator that you are following your passion or going after your dreams is your ability to withstand hardships on the way to fulfilling your destiny. If you are really passionate about going to college, then you will prepare and strive, not accept and survive. My grandfather always likes to say, **"You may be what you are because of your hopes and visions, but you are where you are because of your wise or dumb decisions."**

As I learned during high school with the help of my parents, one of my passions was communicating with new people and learning to understand them. That is why I naturally gravitated towards language classes when I was planning my freshman course load the night before college started. Due to the time lost 'beaking off' to border patrol, I hastily enrolled in an Advanced French class. I was foolish enough to think that I could pass this class in my first semester, even though I couldn't conjugate the verb "aimer". Thinking that my Canadian high school French was superior, I assumed my French vocabulary was acceptable for college standards. Also thinking that I could ignore the course book suggestions of how to take Beginner French Grammar, I impulsively jumped into a French creative writing class. *Mental note to self:* you should only be in an advanced language class if you understand what the professor is saying in the first three days! But hey, university was fun and I thought I would love the challenge, because Lord knows trying to convince student loans to actually give me my student loan money before my first midterm was not challenging enough for me.

In one of those French classes (which I quickly discerned I was ill equipped for), I gained an inner joy as I was sipping my delightful new addiction: vanilla latte. The sweet intoxicating java was laden with sticky caramel that slowly swirled around my tongue and lingered on my hardened pink lips, chapped from walking outdoors in winter to each of my classes. The senior Political Science majors quickly informed me, while I was young and impressionable, that coffee would one day become more needed and valuable than my student loan! I learned to talk freely with seniors while waiting in yet another long line at the campus coffee shop, asking important questions like which coffee got you through Calculus without a nervous breakdown. If one does not think that question is important, they have not watched the movie *Hoodwinked* with the coffee-drinking squirrel.

I savored each joyful sip while trying desperately to wake up and comprehend my French professor. Unaware that I was sipping my coffee loudly like a redneck boyfriend who has horrible soup-slurping habits, I was intrigued by the university professor's lack of concern for memorizing text. They preferred student participation over textbook knowledge. This was an exciting new concept for me! I had never taken a French oral class where we were expected to speak the language being studied. The most 'participation' I learned during my first three weeks of university, was to submissively agree with the local sheriff that speeding and engaging in reckless behavior was indeed very inappropriate. Why he thought I would be a ring leader that he needed to keep an eye on was beyond me!

As I analyzed my teacher's eyes, I could see that she was passionately engaging in lively French conversation with my attentive classmates. She was a petite young woman draped in a soft pink satin dress, wrapped in a fluffy angora mauve sweater that complimented her caring brown eyes. As a professor's assistant from France, she spoke kindly as though each word needed to be whispered; the students in her motherly care were treated delicately. It was a memorable encounter.

Trying to engage the students to respond in proper French sentences, she asked some young women sitting in the back of the room, "What do you think about university?" The young beautiful blond girl that she was looking at intently only gazed with a stern and fatigued face. In the midst of an awkward silence, the student eventually announced passionately, **"La route de l'université est comme un long chemin en enger!"** *(The road to university is like a long road to hell!)*

Hoping and anticipating the startling sentence was merely lost in translation, the rest of us waited for an explanation. Knowing that it was quite common to hear newly-arrived Chinese students ask for a "squirrel" (square root) for their quadratic formula in Calculus, we thought... maybe...? "Are you having fun here?" the assistant blankly inquired. She looked sympathetically into the troubled eyes of the jaded student, to offer reassurance in broken English.

The translation did not concern me, because my best friend had told me about the stressed engineering student she saw at her college, standing on the cafeteria table shouting that he was an 'inverted integer'. I was one of the caring few who would offer sympathy to exhausted students, reminding them to get off the chairs and tables if I had to, by exclaiming, "Hey buddy, get down—the university will make you pay for that, and you can barely afford your calculator!" The only way to reason with engineering or philosophy students that want to be "one with the mathematical universe", is to remind them that the university will make you pay for each of those thoughts, so it might be best not to have too many.

University was intoxicating, yet excruciating; and freshman year seemed to be a hurling roller coaster of all emotions. *If only I had a senior who could help me get my act together,* I thought. Every one of my classmates always looked so "put together". Then as more students sobbed on my shoulder, I realized that no one was as put together as I thought. If you have met the rare person that is… give them a message for me: *"You big, bold-faced liar!"* However, I dare you to find that person—chances are you will be looking for a long time. Over the years, I have collected words of wisdom from students who have been through various struggles, and from professors who have great survival advice for college students during any phase of their education. In case you don't have a big brother to teach you STREET SMARTS, there are experienced veterans who can help you and believe in your scholastic dreams.

Dreams, according to the dictionary, are aspirations, goals, and aims.

We as students often avoid the word "dreams", because the perception of dreams is mystical and abstract. In university you have to be so practical, achieve much, and succeed always. God in His infinite wisdom created dreams in people—man or woman, girl or boy. Even with the well-known patriarch Abraham, the Lord told him to look at the sky and count the stars. God took him outside and said, *"Look up at the heavens and count the stars—if indeed you can count them."* Then He said to him, *"so shall your offspring be"* (Genesis 15:5). These stars represented all of his descendents. God put a supernatural dream in a man who was facing physical impossibilities because of old age, and told him that all things were possible.

Perhaps the reason we as university students are often too frightened to dream, is because school is not part of our dreams—or school has distracted us from the dream. University should be a season in your life that defines the dream and acts as a catalyst for other dreams.

Knowing and cherishing your dreams will enable you to create a smaller list of goals you want to achieve while at university.

Goals are not dreams. Goals are steps you take to achieve your dream. Before you attend college or university, it is important to write down your dreams in a journal, at the front of your day planner, or created as a screensaver on your computer. Reviewing your dreams regularly will energize you when you're overwhelmed by college and are tempted to give up too quickly. You need a list of goals that will help you achieve your dream. If you are an athlete, the dream may be to "go pro", but your goals will help you get there. These life and scholastic goals are over and above what you will already be studying and achieving. University does not help students discover their passion.

What do I mean by *passion*?

...What subject do your friends tell you that you always talk about when you're out together? ...What subject just enrages you? ...What subject brings you to tears, agitates you or compels you to action? ... What subject are you unable to 'drop' every time your parents suggest that you do? That is your passion!!

The university is a business-like structure that has hired qualified professors to train you in your chosen field. In that chosen field, your ideas and thoughts about that specific field will be challenged. It is an institution that will help you develop specialized skills to enable you to enter the bottom rung of your career path. It is not an elite club where intellectuals develop your personality, ability to reason, or define who you are, offering you a high paying job when you are done. Your department head is not there to pull up a chair and talk about your passions over a coffee; they are assuming by the age of eighteen that you already know what dreams you want to achieve, and that is why you're attending college.

For example, your third year International Economics class is not the setting in which the professor wants to debate "ethical" political policy. You may also want to avoid telling your American Economics professor, as I did, that a vanilla latté is the definition of an "equilibrium state". You might also want to avoid telling your political professor that the reason young people do not vote is because eating potato chips and watching reruns from the 70s is much more stimulating for them. Both of these comments may result in a significantly lower grade. The readings that the professor wants to discuss, even though that encourages you to talk once again (after the latté comment, you might want to lay low), are the readings that he has assigned you to read. This accepted reality will also help you develop a more enhanced and cherished relationship with your professor. Keep that in mind, and it will keep you in the class.

> ### Survival Tip #2:
>
> *If you fail, your parents will stop paying for your macaroni and cheese. Then you will have to use your own coffee money and sell blood plasma to buy textbooks. It could be a cold and lonely winter without a cell phone or pizza!*

Therefore, when you choose a major, remember that this is the subject you will be researching, discussing, and writing about for the next four months, 20-40 hours per week. There will be classes you have to take and do not enjoy; however, you should be going to a majority of your classes excited and looking forward to the teacher-student relationship that will occur, even if it is detached. **Here's a hint**: *if you are using a calculator to make butterflies on the ceiling in your European History class, this subject may not be your passion!*

You should not be using excessive quotes in your essays to fill the required pages for your essay (although when you've worked 30 hours that week, sometimes there are desperate measures for desperate times). If you enjoy what you are studying, then you will already be reading books about the subject, and you'll be able to write an essay without extensive research.

Please do not misunderstand me: you need to do proper research and document it well. However, your essay should not be based on the one book that you forced yourself to read the night before it was due! A passionate student that cares about the field that they are in doesn't write their entire essay by cutting and pasting paragraphs from an online encyclopaedia. (However, if you are taking Calculus, that might be the exception! I dare *any* student to read on that subject for 'fun'.)

After promptly reviewing your essay assignments, meet with professors to discuss their research expectations. Do not surprise them the day before it's due with your lack of brilliant reasoning skills. You should not have to use all of your energies purely for the purpose of brow-beating professors into giving you *another* extension for your essay, even if your fourth grandma has died in the last seven weeks, causing the greatest, statistically-impossible grief that you have ever known.

Remember, these professors are your mentors for the next four years; therefore some fruit should result from the encounter. **Hint:** *your enlightened experience with your professor and the class should be more than just the realization that your professor keeps late office hours, which technically means you have until 6:00 p.m. to hand in that essay!*

During my first year of university, I spent many evenings struggling with whether or not I was in the right major. I grew up in a conservative town, and attended a church that talked very little about our destiny. Like millions of young people, I had no understanding that God cared about me and needed me. I had not learned that I have a life assignment, and that God was the creator of my talents and passions. Like so many young people, I had to "crash and burn" a couple of times before perusing my proper destiny. It was not until I had stayed in the dorms and loved it that I realized I was a

"people person". I didn't realize until I lived among other students my age that helping them to become street smart—not just "book smart"—was one of my passions. Each night I went from room to room in search of a microwave to pop my popcorn. As I waited for the kernels to burst, girls would often ask for my advice on where to find a good laundromat, how to get their school assignments accomplished with the least frustration, and where to go for cheap snacks. The frightened girls also began sharing their difficulties with me—their dreams and fears. That is how my nickname in university became "Ann Landers". The reason I enjoyed that "nic" is because I discovered, while talking to other university students, that I loved listening.

Listening to people will most likely be part of my profession for the rest of my life here on earth. For some of my friends, the social aspect of university life was daunting and emotionally draining. I, on the other hand, had a passion for listening to other people's problems and giving them practical advice, in order to alleviate their stress. By helping many people over the years to organize their schedules, prepare for a career, decide on a major, learn how to fill out forms, and phone organizations for information and support, **a fire was fuelled in my soul with each successful task.**

When you attend university or college, each task you engage in will be an indicator towards what you love, and what you are talented at. Even the trials that you experience while attending college, whether they are scholastic or not, will be an indicator as to what your passion is. To know what you are passionate about early in life will give you an advantage with your studies. If you understand your passion before attending university, you can take classes that will develop your talents and stretch your thinking, teaching you new perspectives. In university, there will be many trials; make the decision now to keep your passion in life and fulfill your destiny. However, there is a point in time when you do need to escape everyday activities, and ask God to reveal what you are passionate about. What activities serve as a catalyst for a powerful or compelling force to overtake you? I did not know, in my youthful ignorance, that just the daily routine of life will deplete your dreams if you allow it to.

God gave you a specific purpose in life, and your passion is a path that leads you where you should go.

Dreams were not put in your heart to frustrate you, or cause you to become obsessed. They were put in your heart by God to inspire each phase of your life's journey with aspirations, goals, and aims. One thing I noticed most about students that confided in me was that they were scared to dream. Somehow, asking them to dream meant robbing them of all that

they were and knew. As a senior, this concerned and grieved me deeply. How could we spend a minimum of $40,000 to invest in four challenging years of our lives, sacrificing all that we cherish, to finish with emptiness? After I mourned for several months, came the realization that I was mourning the death of my dreams. Somewhere during the years of attending university, I surrendered my dreams and lost them for a very low price.

With the death of my dreams, came the death of all that I am. *As I looked around, I was not the only graduate full of grief.* I was part of a majority of grievers. It is sad to admit, but on graduation day I did not see all that many thoroughly excited graduates. The only ones that were excited were those who stayed on their journey and fought for their dreams, already doing what they loved. Many students, including myself, were pressured by outside forces into choosing degrees that MAKE MONEY. Mentors are wise in giving that advice, because everyone has to pay rent; however, if you hate 80% of your classes, chances are you will hate the career that follows. If people solely decided their future around money or status, everyone would be completely fulfilled by the money they were making and the titles earned. The truth is many are not satisfied and often have a lot of regrets.

When you are teenager or young adult, it is imperative to discover your passion and be bold about what you love. I discovered that in the classes I loved most, I also earned the highest marks. When you're passionate about a specific subject, it is easy to excel and wake up thrilled each morning.

> **God is more concerned about your personal outcome than the amount of your income.**

"WE GET YOU": WORDS OF WISDOM

Pursue the path that your heart desires, because the direction will fall into place. There's plenty of time to change. Usually one has a whole year of basic courses to decide a career. Don't worry about pursuing your profession; pursue that which you love, and your profession will find you.

PATRICK HILGER, B.S. Industrial Engineering, **Purdue University**

Don't pick your major before you go to college. I'm stuck in a profession, but there are other things that I found more interesting afterwards. Keep an open mind. People ought to double major. Get certain liberal arts classes as well as a professional degree. Make sure you understand who you're getting advice from. In other words, don't learn about engineering from an accountant.

Taste the grass on the other side, then you'll be more content in what you do. Get a well-rounded education.

PHIL POINSATTE, B.S. Chemical Engineering, **Notre Dame**
M.S. Chemical Engineering, **Toledo**
MBA, **Cleveland State** – *Currently working for NASA*

I would like to write a book about, "Maximizing your University Experience". This book would focus on how to create the university experience that you are looking for and how to choose the right University for your needs and career development. If a person is looking for a university to be the sum total of all their experiences and lessons of life, it would seem passively simplistic and unrealistic. One must seek truth and strive to live it, chart their destiny and let God secure their footsteps, seek out what is meaningful to them according to who they are in Christ and their individual development. We must choose a university that will nurture us along in the process of becoming. University was only a phase in my life, which pointed the way and gave me the tools I needed to go forward. I am very thankful for all I have learned from my University experience. God is good.

LINDSAY HEIER, B.A., **Franciscan University of Steubenville**
M.A. Psychology/Counseling, **Reagent University**

There are billions of seconds, millions of people, thousands of situations, hundreds of decisions, scores of life paths, and only one of you. That doesn't matter, though, unless you can think in a way that will encompass these ideas. I mean, you must come around to think long term about life. It is the only way to maintain any shred of perspective, thus allowing for more informed decision-making.

CHRIS NAADEN, **Franciscan University of Steubenville**

I am doing what I love, and I am succeeding... because I am doing what I love in the context of God's will and the local church. I am doing this for a greater purpose than myself—to give back to the community where I work and live. The proof of my passion is that I would do this without getting paid!

L. ROGALSKY, Freelance Graphic Artist

Your courses that you are taking in university are laying a foundation for your future career. If you work hard and lay a proper foundation, your work experience will build on your established foundation and will develop your strengths. It is very important to take the right classes that will enhance your future. The biggest shame I saw in university was watching young students who did not think about their future while they were attending school. Every decision you make will affect your future; therefore decide wisely. Do not just take classes because someone suggested that you should. Your classes should be enhancing your future. This is not high school, and each class you will take is expensive!

NITA CARVALHO, former Liberty University student;
Dental Aid Diploma, **Cambrian College**

I am very happy to still find my job exciting, interesting, and challenging at the end of year 36. I consider myself very fortunate for that. I can't think of anything else I would rather do!!

KRIS RASMUSSEN, R.N. BSc, **Queen's University**
M.N., **Dalhousie University**
Diploma Primary Care, N.P., **University of Calgary**

Do not go to university straight out of high school, because you have no idea what opportunities the world holds until you have lived in it.

GLEN-MARY CHRISTOPHER, BSc Nursing, **University of Manitoba**

Figure out what your curriculum requires. Your advisors are not always familiar with your discipline in detail. It is your responsibility to prepare for your graduation. It is your responsibility to make sure you have taken the right succession of courses, and that you have fulfilled the right requirements to graduate, and the right requirements for further studies.

JOSEPH LIU, BBA, MBA, **Andrew University**

My biggest regret from college is not going to college immediately after high school and getting a 4-year degree, and maybe a Master's. I did go to a 2-year school, and majored in Theatre (if you can believe that). It was a waste of time. My parents should have refused to let me major in that, and made me stick to my original major of journalism. But, at age 13, I wanted to major in law enforcement, and my mother talked me out of it—which I think she shouldn't have done, because 20 years later, I majored in law enforcement, which is what I always wanted to do.

My advice to freshman coming in is to major in something that is "true to your heart", and not let anyone talk you out of it. Select a major that you can envision waking up every morning and going to work, and enjoying your work. I've worked a lot of jobs I couldn't stand doing, but someone else thought I should do, or just worked to have a paycheck coming in. I ask freshmen, "What do you like to do as a hobby or in your spare time? Then find a job that is in that field." Then, they will enjoy going to work.

SUZANNE MONTIEL, Criminal Justice Instructor,
Nash Community College
A.A., **Santa Fe Community College**
B.S., **Fayetteville State University**
M.S., Law Enforcement and Loss Prevention, **North Carolina Central University**

My advice with whatever subject you want to study: go and interview people who work in the chosen field. Ask them intimate questions, like how much they make, if they enjoy the job, is there other people I will have to work with, if so which skills do I need in order to succeed. Do not choose a major because the course catalogue sounds exciting or interesting. Otherwise, in the practicum you will be very disappointed if you have not properly researched the course and the career that will follow. In fact, it was during the practicum that I realized that I could not handle working with this many young children, so I quit my early childhood development course at college. A year of school and a practicum later IS NOT THE TIME to research the career. Yes, my advice is to research your chosen profession thoroughly!!!

SHELLY POCHA, Special Needs Childhood Development Diploma, **Canadian University College**

Don't go to university just because it is expected of you, and "what else are you going to do?" Don't go because you are afraid that if you take time off school, you'll never go back. Don't go because all your friends are going. When you go for these reasons, and you don't have a clear sense of what you're called to do, you'll end up getting into debt and wasting a few years of your life on something that won't help you get to where you're supposed to be, and what you were destined to do.

Before spending the time, money, and effort on university (or any post-secondary venture), you need to at least have an idea of what it is that you want to do, and what you need to get there. I would highly recommend taking the time to think and pray about your future before jumping in blindly. Otherwise, you'll get caught up in the system, and graduate more confused and disillusioned (and more in debt) than when you started.

MICHELLE LEBLANC, Honors BSc Psychology, **Dalhousie University**

Hopefully you have a motivation to go to college. Be passionate about learning something in a certain area. Especially don't go to college if you're giving up a certain passion to go.

JOE LESTER, B.A. Theology, **Franciscan University of Steubenville**

A lot of young people that go to university openly admit that "they don't want to be here, and they don't enjoy attending school." Maybe you should not attend university or continue any longer, if that is how you are truly feeling every day that you attend. Know what God's purpose is for your life, and how your education is a part of that purpose!

JENN LINK, B. Comm., B. Ed., **University of Saskatchewan**

I recommend university. How can you go wrong with education of any kind!

ROSE HAMEL, B.A. Social Work, **University of Calgary**

Before registering, find the right academic advisor. Leave no stone unturned!! A bad or uncaring advisor will leave you like a gypsy, withdrawing from classes you hate and even changing majors mid-year! If your academic advisor is hard to get a hold of, drop them. Find the one that will firmly interrogate you. Those are the ones that will find out what you really want from university. Only then can they send you in the right courses. Stick with the advisor that will spend whatever time it takes.

MARY HEIER, B.A. English, minor in Education and French, **Franciscan University of Steubenville**

Emotions serve a purpose. You are not instructed in the Bible to be 'detached'. You are told to be in control of your emotions. As for my advice, pursue the things in life that you would not regret having done, and pursue them relentlessly. What is just as important is weeding out what is distracting you from your passions—otherwise you cannot focus 100%. In the end, you will suffer for being distracted.

GLORY CRAIG, former Education university student (Artist and Musician)

I remember when I realized I was clueless about how the system operated, and that SCARED me. I picked out classes I liked because I did not know which ones I needed. Knowing information about each class before enrolling is your responsibility.

SHARON BEERE, B.A. Linguistics, **Brock University**

I wish I would have heard more words of affirmation from my parents, that my goals and dreams were attainable. Too often, when I told my parents of my dreams and plans, my parents' responses were peppered with excuses why I couldn't or wouldn't see them through. Adults should encourage young people in their dreams; if they are encouraged, young people will likely succeed in their goals and see their dreams realized, and not be among those who spend their lives dreaming about what they could have become.

BILL CRAIG, Cum Laude B.A. Journalism, Cum Laude B.A. English, **Mesa College**

Then the Lord answered me and said, "Record the vision and inscribe it on tablets, so the one who reads it may run. For the vision is for an appointed time; it hastens toward the goal, and it will not fail. Though it tarries, wait for it; for it will certainly come, it will not delay."

- Habakkuk 2:2 (New American Standard)

Remember to save money for rent! *I'll send you a care package; are you attending classes?? Try not to drink so much coffee, you sound a little uptight on your phone answering message! Make sure you sleep, and go to bed early. Be nice to your friends. Stay focused, and don't spend your classes gawking at cute cowboys!*

"MOM" (C. HENDERSON), R.N., **Confederation College of Applied Arts and Sciences,** N.P. (Nurse Practitioner) Lic. Minister, **World Impact Bible Institute**

you are not alone

CHAPTER TWO

College did not teach us to balance a checkbook

No Money, Honey?

As a young bubbly girl, watching the snow slowly melt in the warmth of spring was like watching a tooth slowly being extracted. I longed to see the dreary grey and white surroundings transform into lush greens and violet hues. As a sweet, vivacious girl, I was most excited about selling boxes of cookies for fund raising efforts. As a "phlegmatic choleric" type personality, I endured many evenings at girls club meetings learning to lead in a supportive and "team spirit" sort of way. Cookie sales trumped leadership classes any day! Cookie sales separated the big dogs who like to run and conquer, from the frail shy girls who just wanted to earn badges while patiently waiting on the porch for their prince charming to arrive. On cookie sales day I would wake up early and pester my mother to curl my ponytails, making them hopelessly cute looking, so that I could exude excessive amounts of charm. I remember how she resisted my pleas to use her blush to make my cheeks rosy. She would curl my hair and offer me feeble suggestions about how cookie sales should not be a competitive event, but a caring way to raise funds for an organization that was impacting a young generation. By the age of eight, I had discerned that it was always in my best interest to disguise my competitive streak from my "be sweet to all" mother.

Cookie fund raising was the day I received top scores for the highest sales, reminding all of the hard working businessmen in my neighborhood that I was a compelling, yet charming force to be reckoned with. The only obstacle I had that day was convincing my nervous mother to take me to the girls' club with an empty car, because I hadn't surprised her yet with my goal of selling 24 cases, instead of 24 little boxes like the other girls. *This* was the day I would rise like a falcon and soar over that annoying little girl with red hair and floppy pigtails. Adults were always commenting on how perfectly sewn her badges were, yet we all knew her doting mother had done the work. She, like many other cute little girls, were going to drown in the sea of rejection as people closed their doors exclaiming, "I don't have money for cookies, little girl!"

That year I assured myself that I would not be the recipient of such volatile hostility. I had already learned by grade one how to quickly 'corner the market'. I discovered, after hours of walking up and down the sidewalk, that just being cute was for chumps. So while my mother was waiting in the car and busy praying for my soul to make heaven, it dawned on me that I needed to be more assertive.

Taking a deep breath, I knocked aggressively on one of my neighbor's doors, so that he and his passive wife could not pretend that they were out. The door slowly creaked open to a cautious space, hiding the aging man like a hunched troll protecting his cave. I tilted my head to the left and made sure that our eyes made contact. I knew, once he gazed into my sweet brown almond-shaped sparkling childlike eyes, that his heart would be pricked. He was well experienced in the art of sales, and could smell by my aggressive stance that my spirit would not be easily broken. As the older professional tried to slowly and strategically close the door on my innocent adorable face, I put my foot in the door for a second strike. He was startled and very unfamiliar with the new generation of women being raised. He looked at me as a German Shepherd would try to stare down a yappy Yorkshire puppy.

"Pardon me sir," I sheepishly excused myself, "but before you crush a young girl's dreams... perhaps you should at least let me tell you about my yummy cookies."

Sensing that I was not an ordinary little girl who would sit on the porch watching the big dogs run, he began to calculate his response. He cautiously leaned downward, bringing his face closer to mine as an experienced businessman would in corporate boardrooms. He whispered so that his wife couldn't hear, "Look, little girl, how many cookies do I have to buy to get you to go away?!"

Knowing that I had conquered a big dog, a surge of empowerment swept through my little veins like warm blood on a hot southern day. "If you buy a case," I responded, "I will not cry loud enough for your wife to hear." He handed me the money quickly, trying making eye contact with my mother to chastise her. Since she was still praying in the car and looking for her holy oil that was always on hand for her children, she was not privileged to see his defeated glare. It was an experience that I will always remember fondly, because those were important days of preparation for my college experience.

Often parents and family members will tell you how much FUN it will be to go to college; however, that is the same speech they gave to naïve little girls as they were handing out a box of cookies to sell. When parents use the word "fun", (which they prefer not to apply to themselves), it is to disguise that "there ain't no money, honey" to pay for your field trip!

During one of my semesters, I was sitting in my comfy black chair that was borrowed from my brother, sipping my new caffeine addiction like a professional student. I caught myself staring longingly at my beautiful tabby cat that was quickly becoming my competition for groceries. *'I could beat her to the shiny grey cat dish'* I thought, as I contemplated competing with her for the Friskies cat food. I was out of groceries and had already eaten every last can of spam I could find in my mother's recent care package. For some absurd reason, I allowed myself to be talked into taking home this pathetic kitten, even though I did not have enough money for my own groceries. Her big golden eyes briefly mesmerized me, not thinking about how much cat litter, canned food, and vet bills would cost. It never occurred to me, as I impulsively solved my 'loneliness' dilemma, that owning a kitten would cost the same amount of money as a year's bus pass. It was *so cold* walking that winter, that I recall my frozen long underwear still sticking to my legs an hour after arriving to class.

Money matters in university, and although fighting your feline for cat food sounds extreme, hey—it happens.

Feeling guilty about grabbing my well-fed cat by the ears to complain that she eats better than I do, I began to reminisce about how wonderful dorms were. Sitting in my musty basement suite that I rented dirt cheap (it was right by the river where plumbing was a problem), I recalled how my best friend and I moved into a dorm for our first semester. Some cheerful students asked us if we were coming with them, because they had room in the car for two more students. I was so touched that within a day we were already being invited to join other university students at a social outing. *Woo-hoo, a legitimate outing,* I thought—then they informed us that they were going to sell their blood plasma (which is legal in the U.S.) to pay for their textbooks. Hmmm...I hesitated... maybe next time! Having to sell parts of your body could definitely be why engineering students prefer to be inverted integers. Yup, I ended up doing some crazy things to pay for my textbooks (nothing illegal). However, the pawn shop might know me by name. Just don't tell my mother I pawned most of her Christmas presents (even though my roommate thought the ugly sweater gift from Mom would keep me warm in our freezing apartment).

you are not alone

The natural fixation with parents and students is focusing entirely on getting into university, and they overlook the 'enduring' part of university. *"Just budget!"* was a joke amongst us students whenever our parents said that, because you have to *have* money to be able to budget it. Money is one of the top two reasons for divorce, and I am convinced it is the number one reason for failure in university. I personally think it is a huge reason for suicides in university. I am not a financial whiz... I just know so many students who had to file bankruptcy when they were done.

So the first question is:

> *Should I go to university right away*
> *if I do not have money to go yet??*

Well, maybe you should consider working for a year first. Nothing relieves stress like going to the finance office and paying your tuition right up front! It does not take a rocket scientist to understand some basic financial dynamics that are very important before going to college or university. If a young student creates a debt-dependent lifestyle while attending university, chances are very high that they will continue that debt lifestyle right into their marriage and career. It is best to learn five basic financial principles at a very young age! Financial success will follow a student who learns how to budget, plan, save money, and be content at all times, while pursuing a lifestyle of giving.

The first basic principle is to understand simple budgeting, so that you know the state of your bank account. Yes, of course, it is easier said than done when every time you turn around it feels like someone is grabbing money from your hand in the first month of college, or sitting on you to dig through your pockets to find every last penny to pay for your tuition! There are two simple solutions for that problem: write down in your day planner every expense that has occurred, and become street smart to avoid losing all of your money to the "system". College is a system that not only trains you for a chosen field, it exists to spend your money for you.

It is much easier to consistently budget if you have *three basic tools:* A BUDGET BOOK that you can buy for a few dollars from Stuff-Mart, RECEIPTS that you ask for each time you spend money, and a PENCIL (that is for chewing on while you glare at your roommate for clicking her pen too loudly while she studies). If you are a technological person with a well-equipped computer, spend some dollars on personal accounting software, so that all you have to do is type in entries each day.

There is one basic concept you want to try to achieve that has taken many alumni and students years to master. You want to spend LESS money than you are MAKING.

Less out than in.

Although it sounds simple, for some caffeine-addiction-induced reason not many students are doing it! I personally think the reason is because they get nervous when they start paying for everything, and give up. Some of us fall in the "AVOIDER" category, because instinctively we realize that we are spending more on specialty coffee and salon shampoo than tuition, and do not want to face cutbacks.

If you are financially illiterate and/or in complete denial, consider making an appointment with a bank financial advisor or look for free financial services to the public (in Canada, there are government programs available to assist students). A student does not run up a huge student loan bill, rack up credit card debt, and then graduate with a high paying job, ridding themselves of all financial woes overnight. Usually what happens is debt, divorce, and a life of anguish. Learn now—it is not too late!!

Are student loan debts the Devil Incarnate? They might be, considering that they will barely cover 60% of your tuition. I haven't met one student who isn't working 25 hours a week because their student loans were not enough. So... have you planned *where* you are going to work while you attend school? You will have to work if you rely too much on student loans instead of saving ahead. Yeah, I ignored advice to save money during summer breaks. I just wanted to get out of my small town so badly, I was willing to endure *anything*. I ended up working 40 hours per week while maintaining a full-time course load, resulting in a couple of failed marks. An awareness of financial planning and time management, combined with realistic expectations, would have helped me salvage those grades.

A lack of financial planning will be the vehicle for your failure. The ideal money-saving solution is to live with your parents for the first two years or in the dorms. This choice will save you thousands in rent, and give you time to recruit the right kind of roommates. At least if things are financially tight, there's food to eat in the dorms, and a car that you might be able to borrow (after much begging and pleading).

One of the biggest complaints I have heard, time and time again, was how much students regretted living in an apartment while going to university. On average, give or take current dollar values, changing from dorms to living on your own will cost you approximately *$1500 dollars extra*, just to cover your basic budget. My monthly rent totalled more than dorm rent with food included. Then there is groceries, utility bills and bathroom products. When you live in dorms, even if you are tight financially, you are still allowed to eat, use toilet paper, have lights and a working phone in the hallway. A friend of mine almost got attacked while using a payphone out in the street late one night, because her private phone was disconnected. The only way you should consider living in an apartment is if:

A) You have a reliable, responsible BILL-PAYING roommate;

B) Your parents are able to help you out in a financial crunch;

C) You are disciplined enough to study at home without being nagged.

Once my best friend and I moved into our own apartment, I went from being a 4.0 GPA student to a 3.0 GPA student. Why did we lose our averages so quickly? Simple: college is already stressful, so worrying about rent and bills on top of that distracted us from achieving our goals (not to mention the cable and Papa John's Pizza that we purchased, instead of groceries). Ask yourself one revealing question that will decide if you should have your own apartment before your senior year: *do your parents have to nag you to study?* If your parents are still nagging you at your age to study, you are NOT ready for your own apartment.

Unfortunately, if you are traveling away to school and you have an absolute inability to sleep in dorms, you will dream of having your own apartment your entire first semester. I shared a room with two other girls, and I was a light sleeper. Every hour I woke up to someone snoring or coughing. It became an unwelcome ritual that almost had musical rhythm and melody by the end of my first semester. The challenge in having your own apartment will be coming up with at least $1000 in damage deposits, and the unquenchable reality of coping with everyday life while you are a student. For example, you will have to clean the apartment, furnish the apartment, pay bills at different locations (avoid lineups and parking fees by banking online), and you will have to deal with any emergencies. If it's winter on the prairies, plan on spending 40 minutes before class just to dig your car out of the snow! Lack of financial planning, when you have your own apartment, will result in selling out your future for the immediate.

Survival Tip #3:

If you have absolutely no job skills and flipping burgers would be "a step up", at least work where you can get a free staff meal.

Those jobs come in handy when you have no food; however, if you are really smart you will work somewhere that gives you EXPERIENCE in your field. If you are short on food, offer to work for a senior citizen who lives nearby—someone you can trust who trusts you in return, for the use of their private laundry facilities and possible home cooked meals. Seniors often need help with yard work, dusting, washing ovens and cleaning windows and curtains. They will often gladly cook you a meal if you are willing to take their garbage out for them. Learning to listen to them and initiate quality conversations with the elderly will also help you develop a servant's heart. Make friends with people in your community, and organize community meals that are often much cheaper than eating alone. Sharing is easier than trying to make a full course meal yourself!

A common struggle in university is that parents help you prepare in the beginning, pay for your books and then wish you well. They are often confused and vexed when their child phones home every week! Well, it may be your first extended time away from home, and you will probably have to fight with the phone company after waiting in line for 50 minutes. Once you make it to the counter, you are promptly told to go home and find proof of residency. Proof of residency is a bill proving that you live where you say you do—a utility bill that you haven't received yet with your name on it! Has a senior helped you discover that when you are a student, you will pay for a large number of damage deposits? I think this is because companies know that most students have no money to pay their power and phone bills, and they want a deposit up front to pay for a monstrous bill. All of these mature adult expectations will seem to consume more of your time than the actual studying. I was horrified when I first spent two hours waiting in line for books, only to find out that if you pick the wrong ones you will *only* get your money back if they are in PERFECT condition and the plastic has not been taken off. That is exactly why you need to become street smart at college, and learn to save money.

Saving money while you are attending college is a learned skill.
This is not about simply accumulating money in a bank account; the skill is developed by finding little ways each day to spend less on what you purchase. The art of being frugal is not a strategy your dad invented to get you to stop asking him for money every Friday evening. Believe it or not (if your father will acknowledge that he has children after paying all that tuition), over the past twenty years he has learned the art of budgeting. He has learned to get the most out of every dollar, so that your mother does not sue him for trying to sell you to gypsies to help pay for the rent.

If that did indeed happen to you, I publicly apologize. I personally have only heard it as a threat, when I was trying to convince my father that he was an unsympathetic tyrant for not realizing that *name brand jeans* were worth sacrificing my brother's tuition money for.

One of the greatest ways to save money is to simply not spend money that you do not need to spend!

> ### Survival Tip #4:
>
> *Go to the used book section to buy text books that are used; some professors change books every semester and you won't be able to resell them.*

Oh right, you imagined that you would cherish and keep every book because they all have memories and deep philosophical meaning? That's because your dad hasn't phoned you yet to inform you that he might be burning everything you left behind. Thinking it could stay there for the next twenty years, hidden away in his basement near his workshop, you were hoping he would just ignore your ab-cruncher machine that you used before gaining twenty pounds at college. Your father will have repainted your old bedroom to become his new study in the first semester after you left for college—he needs the room for the new computers he can now afford, since he is not paying your phone bill. You think that your parents are only dreaming of your success when you are eighteen—but the ones that have had more than two children are often really dreaming about how they will convert your bedroom into a new office that they always wanted. Really, they are not that mean—but some family members may not comprehend that you are tossing a coin to choose between buying a piece of pie, or pay for parking. No worries, I'll solve that dilemma... you will never be able to afford parking—go with the pie!!!

Especially... if you have parents like mine, who screen your calls. My parents had four kids in college at the same time! In the span of nine years they spent $200,000 on their children's education.

They would often leave messages on their answering machine such as, *"If you are losing blood at an alarming rate which will cost us medical bills, press 1; if you are calling to tell your parents you love them and then ask for money, press 2; if you are calling because your apartment is burning down, please refer to our family website and we will get back to you as soon as possible".* Come to think of it, I do not recall them ever getting back to me...

As I was walking down the hallway of the university, contemplating whether or not I should write to Dr. Phil about my parents' phone answering message, I overheard students mumbling, "It's our first week of school and already I am behind". Your first week of university will *not* be an orientation week. By the second day, if not the first, you will already have reading assignments and you will be expected to have your textbooks. DO NOT PUT OFF BUYING YOUR BOOKS. If you don't have the money to buy brand new books, find out where the used book stores are, and search the bulletin board for used books for sale. Be ready and be prepared. If your vision is written down and mounted on the wall beside your bed or your computer, you will not lose your focus and you will not sell out your dreams easily.

WHY does that cafeteria always sell the best pie on the day you have no money after buying your books and parking fees? This is the one challenge I have yet to figure out, and one day I hope that wise older man riding on the bus will have the answer. Not to mention—have you noticed that none of the roads at any university actually make sense?! This is so that you will give up in exhaustion, park wherever you can, and go buy that piece of pie that you will have to sell your blood plasma to afford. Any senior will tell you this: DO NOT waste your time standing in the line for books! Stand in line to buy

a parking permit, or purchase one online the moment it becomes available. (BEFORE THEY RUN OUT!) This will save you hundreds of dollars in parking fines, not to mention the 188 hours of community service that some of us ended up doing—because we told the meter guy he should question his meaningfulness to society. Umm... try not to do that; you will not be able to afford your coffee afterward. And—oh yeah, if you didn't get the pie, no worries; go to a large chain grocery store where they offer free food samples every day, and other students (who have a car with gas) will enjoy it as much as you will.

Remember, if you have already capitalized on selling your blood plasma, there is always the food bank for survival. Many students have relied on it, and there is no shame in doing so. Many students do not come from wealthy or middle class homes, and simply do not have extra money for food and all of the little surprise bills that they were not warned about. Just finding enough food to eat and having enough money for a bus pass is a monthly struggle. I remember bringing my mother's care packages over to international students. Once I saw how bare their cupboards were, I realized that I did not have it as bad. I told them they could have most of my care package, if they cooked something funky for me. When you have limited groceries, you learn to invent every funky recipe there is!

Since many students come from homes less fortunate, they do not have all of the money that they need for college. Not all of these students have a choice—they are dependent on student loans to help them with the huge cost of tuition and books, and if there is any money leftover, for food.

Survival Tip #5:

Beware: students loans are given by institutions that want to make money. Ask them if you can pay them out in full when you are done, or if the interest is 'front load'.

The most tragic student confessions I have ever heard are from hard working students, whose credit has been so badly damaged by student loans that they could not recover. Student loan institutions told me that they did *not* receive my paperwork when in fact the forms were sent. Some student loan representatives said that my friends and I missed the deadlines, when we didn't! Take my well experienced advice. Every time you talk to a student loans agent, ask for their name and employee number. Mark their name and number in your day planner on the day that you spoke with them, along with a summary of your conversation. When you send them information—after asking 5,000 questions first—ask for a receipt from the post office, sending it through the mail in a way that is traceable. Fill out the little form that asks them to send you notice as to when they received your forms. READ THE FINE PRINT. YOU WILL HAVE TO PAY IT ALL BACK!!! IT IS A DEBT INCURRED, NOT FREE MONEY. While you have six months of student loan relief, save your money in an untouchable account so you can make a big lump sum payment. Make payment arrangements that you can handle. Will you be making enough in four years to pay back $40,000? Not many of us are... you might want to consider applying for every grant and scholarship that is available, and arrange for a job rather than obtaining a huge student loan.

Talk about money issues with your parents; do not struggle silently and file bankruptcy before telling them. Which, Mom and Dad, may happen if you do not allow your children to talk freely about their stressors at the college they attend. Many students attempt suicide each year around final exams.

> *Suicide is the third leading cause of death among young people ages 15 to 24. In 2001, 3,971 suicides were reported in this group (Anderson and Smith 2003). (References, Anderson RN, Smith BL. Deaths: leading causes for 2001. National Vital Statistics Report 2003;52(9):1-86.)*

Frazzled young students may engage in reckless behavior during exam week, because they feel hopeless. Just because students assure you that they are adults now, does not mean they have the ability to handle the overwhelming pressures of academia. If you do not have parents to talk to, ask your banker if they can help you find a financial advisor. There is also counselling available for emotional needs on every campus. It is up to a student to be proactive, in spite of how they're feeling, to seek out counsel. Some spending addictions are the result of unresolved emotional issues. Often, the stressors in college trigger the need for "comfort food" or "comfort spending". Unfortunately BOTH are counter-productive. Travelling while attending university is educational—but *not* if it is to escape the stress of your financial circumstances.

You might also want to consider relieving stress for the next year by putting away your income tax refund for next year's tuition, even though you and your buddies were planning to snorkel in Florida. You might get eaten by a shark that thinks you smell like pie... put money away in a rainy day account and a tuition fund. How much?? Put away at least $2000 more than you estimated.

Another way to save money is to lower the cost of your tuition. Leave no stone unturned in looking for scholarships! Most of us only know about the ones offered to students with an average of 98.9% (no ramen noodles for them five days a week!). When you look over crisp scholarship application forms, you'll feel like you are competing on a reality show where any minute the door will swing open and you will hear someone say, "YOU'RE FIRED!" **Do not be afraid of scholarships.** I struggled for two years before I heard my aunt complain that yet again the Rotary Club did not have enough student applications. There are many scholarships that go unused each year. Take a day off purely to hunt for scholarships. Talk to the financial office, talk to the dean's office in your major, talk to the registration office, and most of all, go online and save the whole list of scholarships in your 'favorites' file.

TWO WEEKS OF HUNTING DOWN A SCHOLARSHIP IS LESS STRESSFUL THAN PHONING HOME EVERY SUNDAY EVENING TO ASK YOUR FATHER FOR MONEY.

Unfortunately, many students like myself have not always counted the cost and end up using credit cards so much that it requires shocking explanations at the checkout in Stuff-Mart. When the cashier is calling out "DECLINED" for everyone to hear as if it's Monday night football, a really good comeback is to look at everyone and say, "Why the heck did I lend my card to my ex-boyfriend!!!" Then shed a couple of tears, so that perhaps one of the talk-show-watching women might offer you a dollar for coffee. Learn from seniors...YOU WILL LOSE YOUR CREDIT BY MAXING OUT YOUR CREDIT CARDS!!! So many of my friends are now paying more for their student loan and credit card payments than their rent or mortgage. Many of my friends thought that they would magically have money once they landed that great job... then the taxation office and determined loan agents came looking for them.

I have been told by many of my classmates and neighbors who have heard the word 'declined' that it is still possible to enjoy the shopping experience while in college. I have been especially enlightened by single moms who are attending college, that going to garage sales will save you hundreds of dollars yearly. My neighbour, who is finishing a degree in Human Resource Management, gave me ten all-important tips for becoming a successful bargain hunter. She is the garage sale diva of western Canada. There is no wiser garage sale-shopping-shark than her! 'Bargain hunter' is code for a business student willing to emotionally beat down a little old lady trying to supplement her pension income by having a garage sale. Remember, if you are going to crossover to the dark side by joining the hard-core, early-Saturday-morning garage-salers... there is no turning back!

10 TIPS FOR SUCCESSFUL GARAGE SALE-ING:

10. NEVER ARRIVE TOO EARLY. Ruining the host's concentration while they set up tables weakens your bargaining power.

9. REALIZE THAT YOU ARE JOINING A CULT. These shoppers have joined the dark side.

8. EVERYTHING IS NEGOTIABLE.

7. SCORE KITCHEN APPLIANCES from people who have just refurnished by helping them move. If you are a good lifter, you may even get to keep things they don't want anymore, like a microwave! I'm sure the little old lady will offer you the whole lot if you beat off the single mom who is haggling her for new runners that are only four dollars.

6. NEVER SHOW YOUR WALLET. This will put you in a position of weakness. You never want to be the weakest link. Never let your competitors see your vitals and financial stability. Act poor, and you will get your painting for fewer than five dollars.

5. BREAK YOUR COMPETITOR WITH THEIR WEAKNESS. Distract them with cheap running shoes if you are going after the same pair of designer shorts.

4. BE A BARGAIN STALKER. There is simply no shame in that. These streets laden with one dollar lamps were not made for the wide eyed innocent students not willing to haggle. You are 'playing the game'. Either you are 'in' or you are 'out'!

3. FIRST-TIME GARAGE-SALERS should always stick to the classified ads and purchase a map. If you are too cheap to buy a map, rip one out of your phone book, or get one for free from the local tourism office.

2. SET YOUR BUDGET. Never let your competition see that you are willing to spend more than twenty dollars that day. Be discreet, or else that little old lady will sniff you out like a shark coming for the greasy student that ate too much pie!!

1. YOUR VEHICLE IS KEY. Serious garage-salers never start on Saturday morning in a tiny hatchback. NEVER! Experienced shoppers may park nearby in an old beat-up vehicle, to further enhance their "poor" image.

One of the greatest ways to handle your money in college is through the mindset of contentment. If you are trying to live up to a perceived 'image' in college, you will take that into your career as well! *Substance is always more important than image.* Be content with your current situation in life and make the most of it. If you are a student, enjoy being a student and your career will find you. Enjoy your professors, the pie that you finally bought, and the smile from the little old lady for sharing dinner with her.

If more adults were content in life, they would not put so much pressure on their children while attending college. Sadly, some parents will indeed try to live vicariously through you. They will want you to achieve what they never did. College is about your life experience, not theirs! Save your money and either be content with the budget you have, or find ways to increase your income without sacrificing your soul, your grades and your ethics. Often, once a student learns how to handle their money, they become more content with life. There is security and happiness in contentment. It will drive your decision-making to the path you want to be on, rather than your ego pushing you to do things you really do not want to do.

I remember people thinking they were helping me by joking that I would be flipping burgers one day, with my degree. While it's a funny joke to them, continual chiding from friends and family can be wearing on your soul. It can push you to make decisions with your ego, rather than common sense. I soon realized that I must not allow people to speak that way over my life.

Be selective with the people you allow yourself to receive counsel from. If people do not believe in you, don't listen to them! Do not even listen to their financial advice if they continually mock you. They are not protecting your future if they don't prove by their words and actions that they believe in you.

Lastly, it is never too late to start giving. When you learn how to save, you can also find ways to give. During my second year of university, I found an financial advisor in my church that was willing to allow me to invest just $25 a month (most agents will not allow you to do that). He believed in me, and I will always be thankful for that. He also gave me strong financial advice and reminded me to always be thinking of my future. That is why I started investing while I was attending university. I was investing in my life! He also taught me to give into my future and the future of others. I watched him give to God and continually bless others. His giving lifestyle spoke more to me than his credentials did. When you invest in yourself and respect your future, you will begin investing in others. Your attitude will change from being self-aware, to becoming more community-focused.

I also want to give back to the people who helped me achieve my goals, and be able to give to people who just need one person to believe in them. I want to be a giver the rest of my life, not a selfish taker. It is a lonely, deserted road that the taker is on. When you learn to give rather than take, your reasons for saving and spending money wisely will change. You discover that your finances are not just about you. Success with planning a future and properly learning to budget income will bless all of those people you are assigned to help.

"Taking" leaves people lonely, not being alone. People who have a vision and a strong desire to help others are rarely as lonely as self-absorbed career people. Being a giver also attracts other people who give, and those who have a vision. That new relationship dynamic will be a catalyst for your success. One day, when the taker has no one to call for help while sitting on a hospital stretcher in the emergency room, they'll wish they had given more than they took from their community.

"WE GET YOU": WORDS OF WISDOM

Student loans do need to be paid off eventually. It's not free money. But if you keep going to school, they don't have to be paid off.

ROB BUSCH, B.S. O.L.S. - Organizational Leadership Supervision, **Perdue University**

Always keep an eye out for scholarships. You may qualify for scholarships or bursaries, even if you don't think you do. Dig around to see what your university offers, and apply for EVERYTHING. Also, check out scholarship websites—you can build a profile of your interests, study fields, etc, and will receive info about scholarships applying to those interests. Get some reference letters written, and get busy. Cheaper tuition is not far away!

ANDREA, studied Music, **University of Saskatchewan**

If you have caring parents, listen to them! They have your best interests at heart. If they don't beat you, starve you, or have too many unknown visitors in and out, then they are healthy enough to listen to. Later on in life, you'll wish you had taken their advice!

T. LIGHTNING, **Secondary Education**

The 3 biggest things are: study, be disciplined, and control your finances. There were so many that burned out. The party life was too extreme. I went to OU Ohio University in 1970. We were the #1 party school in the country. A lot of students flunked out after the first semester. They blasted all their cash and never came back. The freedom was too much for new students. Managing your finances is important. Students are out there spending Mom and Dad's credit card. Learn to manage your credit cards and check your balances online.

MIKE BOGGS, B.S. Business and Electrical Technology, **Ohio University**

Don't work full time and study full time. At least not in your first year!

CHRIS, B.A. English

You have to pay your own bills. You take care of rent. It's the first time you're away from home, so your grades flop until you learn how to be your own parent, and organize your time wisely. Always be wary of "the freshman 15". It was the lack of exercise that did it. You can actually live on Ramen Noodles, 10 for $1.

PATRICK HILGER, B.S. Industrial Engineering, **Perdue University**

Don't clean the coffee pot with a toilet bowl brush.

CHUCK, Fabrication Shop Supervisor

Check the library before you buy your books.

K. GLASS, B.A. English

$30,000 isn't a lot of money as a starting wage. It doesn't make you rich.

ERIN KONZ, M.A. Speech & Hearing, **Indiana University**

Budget well, don't eat out, and learn to love all the various gourmet recipes you can make with SPAM.

JOHN MICHAEL STEVENS, Anatomy & Cell Biology majors

Don't use credit cards. We've abused credit cards in the past. We're still paying it off. It's a debt I still wish I didn't have.

DAN CRAIGHEAD, Automotive Industry

Yeah, well, my standard of living is one where it takes $6K a month to break even, let alone eat. If I don't think long-term, I will go crazy. I'm still the man.

CHRIS, B.A. English

Don't make a person-to-person phone call. I called my best friend down the hall, and had a $30 phone bill. Trust your instinct. Follow your heart. If it doesn't feel right, don't!

MARCY WATTS, B.S. Education, Grades 5-9 Language Arts and Social Studies, **Indiana University in Bloomington**

I wish I would have known what clubs and groups were out there. As for Student Services: I was too shy to ask for the things I could get help with. When I went back as an adult student, I got my papers read for better grades. They helped me with employment. University is a little community. Unless you seek help, it won't come to you. I wish someone would have let me know about awards and scholarships. Registering for classes is crazy. The people that could help you weren't available. You have to seek them out. Get a safe walk to your car after night classes. There are book sales as a freshman. Buy used books. You can grade your prof online. You can check out what other students say about that prof online. The bottom line is that you must actively search for your needs. Don't be afraid to ask for help, because if you don't, you will be in trouble!

LAURA HERAUF, B. Ed., **University of Regina**

University did not teach me that you will go to class and then only have two huge exams that decide whether you pass or succeed in your career. University was not at all similar to high school, where I was used to having to do many assignments. Although all those assignments were difficult, the grade was not worth so much, so doing poorly on one did not have the same impact as doing poorly on your university midterm. I was not prepared for the stress that it puts on you. Make sure you investigate alternative options to buying expensive dental tools that you will never use. Those tools are incredibly expensive, and to find out that you did not even use them, or you could have bought them through a different wholesaler is very unnerving. Search out ways to save money in your program!

SHANDY LAGLER, BSc Dental Hygiene, **University of Alberta**

Don't mooch off people. I had a rich roommate. Then you realize that you're taking others for granted or using them. Don't be the moocher or let others mooch off you. People begin to take you for granted or dislike you, or you dislike them.

JULIANNE BURT, B.A. Music Education, **University of Dayton**

Find what you like; and do what you like because it's really hard to change careers once you start. Don't chase the easy jobs when you get out of high school, if it's not what you really want to do.

KEVIN SIMON, B.S. Math and Computer Science, **Lawrence Technological University**

If you were a class clown in high school, don't steal the show in university! People actually spend money to go there. "Better to keep quiet about your ignorance than to speak up and remove all doubt!" University is a time of poverty. Lock up anything that may be worth over $75. Your roommate's friends can be the worst thieves. If your roommate steals, forget politeness—move out immediately.

MARY HEIER, B.A. Education, **Franciscan University of Steubenville**

Now that I am looking at university from my kids' point of view, I do not think that they are ready for all the things facing them. It is different now, than when I went to college. The world in which they live in is different. They will feel ready to handle university just like I did, but it is me that feels differently. I feel now that I have to look out for them.

KATHY WYSZOMIRSKI, Certificate in Health Administration, **University of Saskatchewan**

I should not have bought every textbook that was "required." Some such "required texts" were hardly used and were available to borrow from the library if needed. I found out later the value of talking to upper year students to determine whether or not the suggested text was really a valuable asset to the course. In addition, I wish I had looked into buying used textbooks instead of immediately snatching up the fresh, glossy texts that bore exorbitant prices.

JAMES, BSc, current Medical Student

Don't get a credit card. Don't have a full time job if you can. I had two jobs that equaled 50 hours a week. I was so tired from work that I started skipping classes. Live in the dorm your freshman year.

KIM LYMAN, B.S. Management, **University of Bloomington Temple University**

The daycare center I worked for paid for my psychology classes. The classes were really good, because I went through two different colleges, and both in Connecticut were in Bridgeport. I was in Danbury, so location was close. A prof even came into the daycare. It was convenient and free. I proved to myself that I could take a class and succeed, because I ended up with a 4.0 GPA.

LINDA DAVIS, B.A. Psychology, **University of Sacred Heart St. Joseph's College**

Don't get a credit card. Do NOT do it. You'll spend it on beer and cigars. That's what I did. They don't explain the 19.5% interest rate. You DO have to pay it back.

ANDREW KLUSMAN, B.S. Marketing, **Franciscan University of Steubenville**

Go live in housing/dorms to meet other freshmen, rather than going with random older people. Then the next year you can choose roommates that you know.

RICK, B.A. English

Don't adopt pets if you are thinking about traveling all summer (unless you have very nice parents).

MARIE-LYNE, BSc
M.S. in Veterinary Medicine, **University of Saskatchewan**

Don't get pregnant, or get any one pregnant.

NATALIE, BSc Vet Medicine

Don't listen to the lies that credit card companies tell you—going into debt is the DEVIL!!

STEPHANIE STRIPLING, Studying Comparative Literature

Don't take more loans than you need, because it will come back to bite you. I was a non-traditional student, I already know how to make my way around and stay organized. It was just finding enough time in the day to do what I had to do. Having learned the hard way by not having a degree, I learned the value of having one; do not treat the experience lightly. It opens doors and options that otherwise wouldn't be available.

ADAM GOLD, B.B.A. - Business Administration in Accounting and Computer Information Sciences

University didn't teach me how to balance a checkbook!

BILL BOGAR, B. Comm. - Commerce & Finance Accounting & General Business, minor in Computer Science, **University of Saskatchewan**

Live at home and go to a local college, *at least for your first two years. It's called "Debt Free" college. When you stay with your parents, they're better able to guide your choices for a future partner. You are also able to stay with your family longer, which makes you a more balanced, mature individual. That is, if your home life is healthy. Staying up late at night is not worth it. Your body is more susceptible to colds, even if it is for studying. Nothing good ever happens past midnight. When you make money, living at home, you can save for a car or house, and start off life or marriage on a more solid footing.*

TERESA LESTER, B.S. Elementary Education, **Franciscan University of Steubenville**

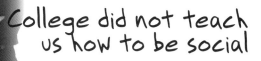

CHAPTER THREE

College did not teach us how to be social

Care to Connect

I distinctly remember being five years of age when I decided I needed to take the Calgary city bus home. My older siblings, I thought, were too late picking me up, leaving me alone in the playground way past closing. So I clutched my change and told myself I could get on that monstrous bus! As the bus roared closer to screeching halt, the clattering doors swung open as though a vacuum was shaking my little body. The sheer force of air on my fragile face caused me to step back. With a loud husky voice I heard the bus driver yell, "Are you getting on or not?" I just couldn't step up onto that bus. I decided instead to shuffle home in shame. I was more distressed by my inability to conquer the city bus, than I was by my loneliness. When you are five years old, the walk home alone in a big city is a two hour journey during dusk. Upon returning home from work, my frantic mother sent out a search party for me. I suddenly learned at a young impressionable age that if you do not 'take a risk' and get on that bus, it is a long painful journey home. The next week I became a subconscious protector of other young fragile 'latch key kids' who had to walk home by themselves. There was an innate desire in me to nurture the lonely. It was then that I began my journey as a transformational leader. I was willing to risk my reputation, and all that I knew, to follow a vision and passion that drove me to help the hopeless.

There has been a transition in the academic culture: students view themselves as paying clients, rather than learners seeking ideas. Rapid advancement of technology has fundamentally altered our ability to socialize, because we are dependent on binary code rather than people. University and college both have cultures that develop with the students who attend. Academic changes do not always keep pace with changes in the world. Campuses are like small cities, each with their own unique set of do's and don'ts. It is often this culture that dismays intelligent students from various backgrounds, who are ill-prepared to deal with the emotional and social stressors that accompany their college experience.

Most students just want to go to college, have a roommate, eat some pizza and do well in class. They are not prepared for roommates who steal, sexual predators, having to handle grade disputes professionally, obeying campus police, and learning proper formal rules when addressing deans and faculty. In short, they may be spending more time in their first year trying to learn the 'new rules' than they do studying.

A wise science major from my university, stated that *"you will do university the way you do life"*. This is why gifted high school students, who have been allowed to be socially independent, will not be able to hold interesting conversation with future classmates. The ability to engage in meaningful dialogue with college peers comes from sharing and caring about others' life experiences. Students lacking social skills will be lost in the raging sea of cyber technology, overwhelmed by the size of their campus, while trying desperately to discover where they fit. They will feel as though no one seems to notice them.

During a commerce class assignment, my work group agreed that conference calls would work better with our schedules. We addressed the details by phone and online, sending emails back and forth to the professor for feedback—never once introducing ourselves in person. The result of this new style of cyber-communication is advanced efficiency, yet greater loneliness. One would think that with all of the technological advancements, students would feel a greater connection; yet more and more students are feeling lonely and lost. The only way that most students overcome this social disadvantage is to go out of their way to be involved in clubs and cultural organizations that their degree is relevantly affected by.

> **Learn to simply smile and genuinely care about others, and other students will gravitate towards you.**

It is always surprising to observe in a large university full of many social clubs, some university students dropping out because they are lonely. When the average student is studying in high school, they may have a perception of college based on what they see on television. They think that the minute they arrive on campus, they will be surrounded by new friends with invitations to parties, not realizing that socializing in college is very similar to high school. The same social skills that a young person has leaving high school, is the same social skills that they will have entering college. The intense rapid pace and added pressures that students feel, will heighten or reveal possible character flaws that were easily disguised while living with their parents.

I was very shocked to be informed by my roommate that I was sleep-walking. She had to come to fetch me out of the shower that I was taking fully clothed; the stressors of college had triggered my sleep-walking tendency. She did admit that it freaked her out—but considering that I was the only friend that could wash dishes as perfectly as this 'oldest child in the family' could, we decided to call it even!

When a student enters college, they are better able to handle the social and scholastic pressures if they are friendly and willing to try something new. I am not talking about wild abandonment; introduce yourself to classmates, or join a club that you might not have tried joining in high school. Every year during the first week of college, there are usually many clubs advertising in the hallways or announced in the classrooms. Joining a club at the beginning of the year has many advantages: seniors are more willing to help freshmen that are 'in their club', and it's a great opportunity to meet other students that are as neurotic as you are.

Survival Tip #6:

In order to have friends, you must be a friend.

This is truer in college than it ever was in high school! Often these social clubs have connections to summer employment opportunities and travel experiences. If you are shy, join a university club and on your way each night, think of possible subjects you could bring up to get people talking. A great ice-breaker at the debate club is starting an argument about who is better: Winnie the Pooh or Tigger (it resembles the 'senate versus congress' debate to me). Discussing slushies and flavors of slushies is always a classic. My point is, RELAX; it is not that hard to talk to other students. Just remember, they are all under pressure like you, and they all need someone to genuinely care about what they say. Look at them when they are talking, and listen. Don't give them advice; just care.

Sometimes all it takes to make your day brighter is seeing someone smile kindly at you in the hallway. According to most researchers, it is common knowledge that over 90% of communication is non-verbal.

Look for cues as to how you should treat someone when you are talking to them at college. Is your professor or classmate crossing their hands and legs while they are talking? This means that your tone or conversation is threatening. Pick up a book on non-verbal communication in order to understand how you appear to others, while you are speaking. Are you talking to new people the way that you would want to be talked to? Are you crossing your arms or tugging at your hair while looking at the floor, when talking to a new classmate? These skills are important because you will be asked in college to join many more group projects than you experienced in high school, with one major difference. In high school, the teacher intervened if your group was not getting along! This will not occur in college, where the professor will only suggest you do an entire 12-page project by yourself as the alternative.

Hint: *No one in college that is maintaining higher than a 'C' (2.0 GPA) average has time to do an extra 12-page project by themselves!*

You will not only need to work effectively as a team member and engage in productive communication, but also lead and facilitate projects while earning your group's respect. By the time I entered my senior year of college, I quickly realized that buying specialty coffee and cookies for my work group did more for our negotiations, than any textbook leadership technique ever will! If you're not getting along with your group members or are always being ignored, try the coffee approach. Vanilla lattés are a good choice that most people appreciate, or offer to do a coffee run on your own time. I have never met anyone yet that has been angry with me for helping them to relax, while we work out plausible solutions. You will also get higher participation marks from your professor when she sees how happy you make your team.

Some of these group members may turn into long term friends, and some will be a passing exposure to new personalities. Allow room for either experience in your life. Some people are simply not destined to be best friends—and if you are a social butterfly like I was, you must learn not to take that personally. It is perfectly normal not to retain friendships with every acquaintance you've made in college; but your life after graduation will be enriched by some of them!

Don't think that the professor is oblivious to your participation in a class of fewer than 100 students. The professor is merely forcing you to adapt to a more realistic work environment by not rushing to intervene every time a team miscommunicates. Learn to address some basic delegation matters by email, saving your time for putting the project together and ensuring that the essay flows properly. It is awkward to read different writing styles within a group essay, and may result in a lower mark. I recommend that your group assigns a member who can edit well, and someone who can design an eye-catching cover, while ensuring a consistent typestyle. It is advantageous to do background research to get extra marks for the assignment. The extra information and stylish presentation is what makes the difference between an average group project and 'the best in the class' group project. Make sure your group properly defines what the professor wanted, and surpass those expectations. Have a group checklist, marking off each requirement with a checkmark. When you're in college, it becomes *your* responsibility to ask questions. You must seek out your professors, administrators and classmates.

Do not wait for one of your group members to call you; take the reins and ask them at your first meeting for full names, phone numbers and email addresses. Phone them relentlessly if they are being negligent. Your group needs to have total participation, not students letting the other group members do everything. If you are dealing with foreign students who need help translating their material, delegate their portion of the assignment as soon as possible and always have the group editor review their work. I have personally studied five languages, and realize how difficult it is to have perfect grammar in a second language. Those computer language translation programs do not always catch slang or cultural nuances.

Make sure you also talk slowly to foreign students and ask them politely if they understood everyone. Do not embarrass them; just ensure that they were not simply nodding because they were so overwhelmed with the group's rapid conversation. Not only will they be thankful for your kindness, but they will be able to give you valuable research and group participation that you need. It is important to learn how to value each team player, regardless of their major. Most graduates have difficulty when they enter the work force, because co-workers and bosses are not as forgiving or willing to negotiate as much as your understanding classmates will. Functioning well within your group project will help you avoid feeling lonely, isolated, and frustrated.

Loneliness is not due to the absence of friends, it is due to an absence of vision. When you are a dreamer that is pursuing your dreams, you probably won't feel lonely. Dreams and visions push you to work hard and stay focused, with a desire to help others fulfill their dreams. My friends would always tell me that I should get paid for the advice and help that I gave them; however, when you help others realize their dreams you will be helped with your own. If you are a Political Studies major, phone the office of any elected representative and offer to volunteer. You will not only get your feet wet, but you will find your own rare breed of "neurotic obsessive compulsives" who think like you do about the fundamental necessity in road planning budgets! If you are a Fine Arts student, try out for a play in your first semester. Why not? What have you got to lose? If you're not selected for the play at first, you might be less nervous auditioning the next time. The point is: GET YOUR FEET WET IN THE AREA YOU ARE STUDYING right away. You may discover that you do not even want to be in that major! Being exactly like your classmates is not an indicator that you're in the right major.

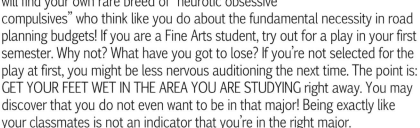

The biggest detriment I observed with unsuspecting students was falling victim to stereotyping. Just because you do not wear glasses and drink pop from a can does not mean you are ill-suited for the math department. You may very well end up as the dean of that department one day if you are more charismatic leader than your classmates. Allow yourself to be who you are, and develop the skills that you know you have. Do not allow stereotypes to make you second-guess your social or academic skills. Not every English major has to become an unsocial, brooding, dressed-in-black scholar to achieve success in the literary community. This false expectation will also get in the way of becoming friends with people who "do not fit your world". My mother always used to remind me that, "Kindness does not have a world."

Kindness can be offered to anyone, and everyone deserves kindness.

Many students who are my age and younger have come from a daycare background. The daycare generation has come of age, and approximately two out of three students have been in daycare. Some grew up as "latch key" kids (who took care of themselves until a parent returned from work). The daycare system did not reward those who came from homes with financial stability; the system was defined by those who could socially prevail. The children that became weaker in the social environment of a daycare were the children who could not adapt to the group dynamics.

It is not surprising that my generation related to shows like *"Friends"* and *"Survivor"*, compared to the family sitcoms that my mother adored growing up. In the daycare environment, we grew up with security coming from our relationships, not authority figures. Most of us came from single-parent homes in the 70s, during the beginning of the women's movement. Often, children learned to seek protection and nurturing from the larger, charismatic kids. We were the ones with power and influence.

This daycare generation is now graduating from high school and entering the demands of modern university. Although the term "Daycare Generation" does not explain rapid change, it does explain to a large extent why young students are reacting to the changes in college circles, workplaces and modern stressors that are present. The result of this daycare culture is a greater need to assimilate. Now of age, the daycare-raised generation is facing dysfunctional pasts, integrated families, stereotyping of a new kind, and rapid technological and political changes. *"This is not our parents' Oldsmobile!"* Our daycare childhood does explain our adaptable lifestyles with a desire for revised work hours; hence the rapidly growing trend towards home-based small businesses.

In my teens and young twenties, I watched President Reagan end the Cold War, the wall come down in Germany, the collapse of socialism in Russia, Desert Storm, the development of the Internet, and now the "War on Terrorism". Progressive change is indeed normal, but my friends and I have watched all of this occur in just sixteen years. That is a magnitude of political and economic change within a very short impressionable period. I majored in Public Administration, and within our department, students were not sure how to write their essays because the political sphere seemed to change every 15 days. By the time our essays were due, our research was irrelevant because the United Nations was no longer supporting the nation we had recently written about. We are not at all like our baby-boomer parents, who wanted to simply work hard and find retirement with dignity.

We seem to be a generation with an entirely different world view and a greater capacity to take risks.

Survival Tip #7:

Your social life will only hurt your grades if you are reckless and value it more than your classes.

One of the comments I've heard from many students over the years was that they are still close to friends that they attended classes with. That is so true!! Most of my closest friends attended with me, united because we had "common ground". It is like a secret alumni understanding. The friends you make in college will most likely be friends for life, which is precisely why you should choose your friends wisely. Socializing should be one of the great highlights! It often disturbs me to hear of students that rarely socialized. What an absolute shame, to go through four long years of college and not take the time to care about a friend.

Friends will either enrich your life or help destroy it.

If you are wise in choosing who you associate with, you'll be challenged and nurtured by other students with different social backgrounds and age experiences. One of the ways to enjoy friends is to include them in some of your college experiences. Go to a funky café with an international student, bring a friend to the gym with you, or offer to do laundry at the same time. If there is little time to socialize, socialize on the way to class or during other daily tasks. Shop for groceries with a friend, rather than text messaging about some 'hottie', while noticing the firefighter's cute butt near the apple stand.

I have talked to many students who did not even realize what was included in their tuition until after they graduated. I didn't realize that I was paying for a membership at the university gym, the entire time I was attending. Let me tell you, I put on so much weight in college, I felt like the Michelin tire man— I could have used that gym! Find out what is all included when you register. Get a list of all the social clubs and school clubs. Be bold! If you are good in sports, try out for one of the teams. Just manage your time well. **Socializing does not hurt you—lack of time management does.** Being social expands your networking ability to function effectively with professors and administrators. A social life will enhance your education in many ways; good social skills are developed over time.

Students who work twenty hours a week, study twenty hours a week, and attend classes faithfully, need a stress release on the weekend. That is why it's important to pick your friends wisely—they are the ones who will influence you to engage in constructive or destructive behaviour. There will be times that you'll feel 'you just need to get away from it all'. Reputations are very hard to repair once you are in college, because colleges are like small towns with their own cultural nuances. **Hint:** *If you want to be respected as an intellectual, it might be best if you don't go to parties with your professor, or get caught vandalizing school property by the dean.* "Is this not common sense?" parents are asking. Uhhhh… this tip is not common sense to a drunk college student trying to forget their Calculus midterm.

Making wise choices under pressure is often the result of seeking counsel from wise people. It has become very popular during all of the rapid social and economical changes, to seek out a mentor. Mentors are very good for young people, because it gives them a visual example of what they could achieve, or where they could be in twenty years. Mentors may not be experts within a student's area of study. However, they may have common characteristics and similar personalities. Many young people are now seeking out mentors by asking professionals that they admire to give input into their lives. Some organizations are offering programs that match young people with selected mentors. Many church ministers are beginning to value mentorship of young people, whether they will be entering the ministry or not.

My generation feels lost, and many are coming from homes they perceive as dysfunctional. A mentor helps to develop a young person's ability to problem solve and cope with life. Consider seeking out a mentor while you

are going to college. Find someone successful within the field that you are pursuing a career, and ask them if they will spend some time with you. Glean every bit of information that you can, looking for opportunities to bless them—DO NOT waste their time. They will not only groom you professionally, but if they miss seeing you slide down a snow-packed hill on a cafeteria tray turned into a sled, they may offer to be a well-needed reference for you. Having a mentor will also remind you to avoid reckless behaviour, because you need a reference and a job when you are finished college.

Often students have confided in me, with tears in their eyes, explaining that they cannot understand why they habitually engage in reckless behaviour. They just felt like they were going to 'snap' and needed to get away. What they really needed was someone to talk to, not speeding in their boyfriend's yellow hot rod down the city freeway under the influence of narcotics. In my years of attending college, I have met so many students who made the honour roll in high school, never once defying the rules; and then became drug addicts during college. I was surprised by how many students I knew that could not go longer than five days without alcohol or stimulants.

If you find yourself engaging in reckless behaviour and handling relationships very poorly, consider going to a free counselling clinic that is usually available at colleges. Often poor behaviour and dysfunctional pasts seem to creep up on students when they face new pressures. Issues that were thought to be swept under the rug successfully, come out of nowhere. If you have some unresolved conflicts in your past, or silenced assault experiences, they will surface when you least expect it. I remember breaking down in tears while writing a French final, as I was trying to assure the people around me that I was fine and the grammar was not that difficult!! Ministers, priests and college counsellors often offer free counselling, and they are very compassionate in helping you resolve emotional problems that resurfaced when sharing an apartment with a roommate that is a neat freak just like your ex-boyfriend!!

Survival Tip #8:

What kind of social life do you want?
Decide before you enter college!!

Many students have no idea what to expect when entering college. All they've decided is to have freedom, and finish a degree or diploma that gets them a good-paying job. If you are a high school student, write a list of goals that you want to achieve while in college—without having to sacrifice everything to attain them. Often there are three common social expectations of students: they want to find their soul mate, they want future business connection, and they want friends that "get them". Often at college, young men and women are hoping to find their lifelong partner, and are discouraged if they do not.

I remember when I went to Bible school, all the girls referred to it as 'BRIDAL SCHOOL'. This term was a very accurate joke. Many students do get engaged in college. There is nothing wrong with that, IF you are improving and achieving goals together. Some couples that got married in college improved their average and became stronger students, progressing together as a team. Some students became pregnant, dropped out of college and ended in divorce.

If you are going to have a serious relationship in college, ask yourself: "Am I mature enough to get married?" Watch the results of your engagement with that 'awesome' girl or guy. If they really are awesome, they won't try to convince you to spend your study time taking them to a dinner and a movie. They will respect your vision and your dreams, and help you achieve them—not use you to advance their selfish ambitions. Does your boyfriend want to spend time with *you*, or is the entire evening spent editing his overdue essay while he plays video games? You may just be his editor for that semester and replaceable after Christmas! If your girlfriend is wanting you to help her with math homework every Monday and Wednesday night before class the next day, you may just be her 'free' tutor. Ask them to spend time that evening doing something else and watch what reaction they give you! If you expose their motives, remember: you are paying money for your tuition—they are not!! Be bold and look for someone who wants to be with you because they truly care about you!

10 REASONS EVERY WOMAN SHOULD CONSIDER HAVING A MALE CAT INSTEAD OF A COLLEGE BOYFRIEND:

10. YOU WILL NOT HAVE TO SING *"All By Myself"* one day with your single depressed friends.

9. When your male cat drinks out of the toilet, he leaves the seat DOWN.

8. YOUR CAT IS HONEST about being scared of the vacuum cleaner.

7. YOUR CAT KNOWS HOW YOU FEEL; he does not care, but at least he knows!

6. Your male cat is not confused about your bedtime.

5. The only time your cat looks at you disapprovingly is when you do not feed him promptly at 8:00 a.m.—not when you are 25 minutes late for every silly appointment he has!

4. Your male cat knows how to whimper, but he does not know how to use the remote control for the television......... he's a keeper!

3. When you are busy, you can make your male cat happy by stroking him, petting and feeding him—and all in under 5 minutes!!

2. When your male cat is getting "under foot" in the kitchen and whining too much, you can appease him with cheap catnip.

1. Your male cat is not secretly dreaming of putting a 57-inch flatscreen television in amongst your Victorian living room furniture!!!

* * * { I was told by young men that they only have two reasons to stay single: One reason is they have money leftover at the end of the month, and the other is that the only whining they have to listen to is from their dog. } * * *

There is great wisdom in making and keeping various connections with others, but not at the cost of using them for personal gain and offending their integrity. Friendships should be genuine and your connections should be based on a 'win-win' philosophy. This mindset ensures that both parties benefit from any idea or project that needs collaboration. If you continually take advantage of people and defile them in the process of getting ahead, it will come back to haunt you one day. My grandmother always told me:

Watch who you kick on your way up, because you may be polishing their shoes on your way down!

This truth is very applicable in college. You may get ahead on one project or steal a paper in one class; however, if you are in a small college or university, word gets out and rumours do travel. I was surprised to see former classmates out in the workforce, waving hello to me with a big smile on their face. After noticing their title, I was *so* glad I had bought them a cookie on our group project! Some of the faces I encountered while paying bills were not so friendly, and it is a shame that I left them with little reason to respect me, now that I am older and more mature. For every stinging word you make to a classmate or roommate, it will take 20 positive statements to rebuild them.

"People will not always remember what you said, but they will remember how you made them feel!" Make no mistake—your attitude and character flaws will follow you into your dream job, which you will be fired from for being such a toad. You really need that first entry-level job; you cannot afford to blow it because of unprofessional behaviour, unable to get along with your co-workers. Learn from people who have made mistakes in college and try not to repeat them! Every relationship you have in college will be practise for handling clients in your professional career.

Finally, college students in their first year are often unable to handle sizable student loans, and the new adult pressures that college brings. The result is one big DRUNK. Many students have failed and dropped out of college because they either spent all their money in the first semester, or they partied so much that their average is irretrievable. Part of this "need to party" is due to the fact that these students crave the social life that they never experienced in high school. Many students develop serious addictions during their college years. If you are waking up the next day with a sock stuck to your jeans, lying next to a guy named 'Ted' (well, that is what the tattoo says) on a futon that you don't recognize, and you can't understand why your cell phone keeps ringing after giving it to your cat to eat the night before… it might be time to reassess your behaviour!

Hint: *If you had no intention of being with Ted, please refer to the top ten reasons to have a male cat instead of a boyfriend in college.*

Let's go over some facts:

a) That STD you just got from Ted will start dripping soon.

b) Your cat did eat the phone, and it is ringing from his stomach (more vet bills).

c) You are too hung over to care that you are eating ramen noodles and vomit for supper tonight.

d) Your party friends don't care about you (otherwise you wouldn't be stuck with Ted right now, because they just stole your car and your credit card).

e) You probably will be spending the rest of your weekend crying and listening to blues music, recovering now instead of finishing your essay by Monday.

f) Silly rabbit—tricks are for kids!

Survival Tip #9:

*Never open a care package from Mom in public.
She always puts personal and embarrassing stuff
in the box!!!*

I remember how excited I was when my mother had sent me a care package as promised. Care packages in dorms were like cigarettes in prison. We would walk down the dorm hall, shouting *"CARE PACKAGE!"* triumphantly, like a runner who had just completed their first marathon. We not only wanted to show our dorm mates that we had parents who still loved us and forgave us for costing so much, but we could also sell some of the chocolate, macaroni and cheese boxes and reading flashlights to the highest bidder. I only experienced one difficulty with my first care package, which I never want to relive. It was a cool crisp spring morning, and I thought the golden rays of sun would be an indicator of good things to come—which was why I was so elated that spring day when I received notice in my mailbox of a care package. I missed my mother and my nation so badly that my stomach ached and my heart skipped un-rhythmically. I could *not* wait; I wanted to see my mother's expression of love wrapped in each present so badly in that frustrating first semester, that I decided to open the box right away in the university mailroom before returning to my dorm to brag to all my friends. **Hint:** *if the box feels heavy, she packed it with too much stuff and you are going to see an explosion that only occurs in action movies!*

My mother was a practical and efficient nurse practitioner who liked to 'kill two birds with one stone'. She decided to pack my fragile package with soft feminine hygiene products to protect anything from breaking. Why not? They would come in handy too! I was young and trusting, so why would I suspect such an outrageous idea? Who would want to do such a thing??

My mom would. Of all my years growing up, I do not recall being as red as I was that day, picking up feminine hygiene products from the mailroom floor, and stuffing them into my school bag because they would not fit back into the tightly packed box, while the good looking football players laughed hysterically nearby. I should not have been humiliated so quickly, and simply waited for them to open *their* box of underwear from their southern momma. I did not wait to open the box that was ticking like a time bomb, and suffered through more laughter than when I accidentally had toilet paper stuck to my shoes.

There is no word or emotion that can explain the conflicting love/hate you have for your mother when you are 18. I walked the hall of shame back to my dorm that black drizzly spring morning, as I questioned whether spending Easter with her was really necessary. *What would she do next,* I thought—*buy me an ugly orange sweater from Stuff-Mart??* (Be prepared: that comes at Christmas, along with a small microwave that you have no room for, because she did not like you eating out so much). I did not speak of that care package again, even though my roommates eyed it suspiciously.

I love my mother, but I had no choice but to wait an hour in the dorm hall to use the phone and demand an explanation..."*WHAT WOULD POSSESS YOU TO DO SUCH AN UNTHINKABLE ACT??! WHAT HAVE I EVER DONE TO YOU??!!!*" I spent that evening assuring my mother that the care package explosion was much worse than when she spit on her finger and wiped my face in front of my boyfriend. Mothers say that they are doing things for you because they care, but even angelic mothers can be 'passive-aggressive' in punishing you for leaving them. They could also be mad if they saw your best friend wearing her Christmas present that you pawned for a chocolate bar. Be careful; always second-guess your mother's behaviour while you are attending college. It is not normal to pack care packages with unmentionable products. If you want an engaging social life that allows you to hold your head up high in the dorms, BEWARE OF MOM!!

This is the one defining moment in which fathers are redeemed:

In spite of Dad's military chant—"get in, get out, hustle... hustle... hustle!!!" and in spite of the aloof card that he sent only because mom made him; in spite of Dad's relentless nagging, his suggestions to move back home, and his lectures about how responsible *he* was when he was your age (which Grandma told you was "all a pack of lies"); Dad would *never* in all of his financial or vengeful ways even think for one moment that it would be normal to send an embarrassing care package!!

That, my friend, is why we will ALWAYS LOVE DAD!!!!

"WE GET YOU": WORDS OF WISDOM

The students who I have found were successful were the ones who had good communication skills coming into college. The deck is stacked in colleges in favor of those students who value and utilize communicating well. That is understandable because corporations now in amongst globalization are seeking out graduates with those skills. The middle class is eroding and the pressures in college are more real, so too is the competition. The students who have good communication skills are going to be the ones who survive and succeed within that kind of pressure.

DR. SUSANNA HORNIG PRIEST
B.A. **University of California, Berkley**
M.A. **University of Las Vegas, Nevada**
Ph.D **University of Washington**

University is not easy; however, it is a unique once-in-a-lifetime experience for every person. Enjoy all aspects of the journey: the professors you like and dislike; the classmates you hope to remain friends with, and others you hope have dropped out; the commissioners who sit at the entrance to the library and always say "Have a good day"; the department secretary who makes you feel that your question is not ridiculous; and the Department Head who really does not eat first year students for lunch. All of these people play very minor roles in your university experience; yet they do alter how you approach your future in ways you may not even be aware of. When the journey ends, whether it is 3 years, 4 years, or 10 years, the most important thing that you can do for yourself is attend Convocation. That is when you realize just how much you have achieved.

CAROL ROMANOW, RN, B.A., M.A., **University of Saskatchewan**

Play hard and study hard. I played a little too much in the beginning. Have a structured lifestyle. Make yourself schedules.

GREG FRY, B.S. Political Science, **University of Maryland**

Do not jump on a stop sign that has fallen over and is lying on the ground. My flip flops were slippery that day, and now I have a discolored bump on my leg that won't seem to go away. Also, do not play scavenger hunt with your roommate's shoes if she has an interview that day or an important meeting. Only hide her shoes in the fridge when you are both bored.

Lisa Nagelmakers, B.A. Communications, **Wilfred Laurier University**

I wish I would have known what clubs and groups were out there. As for Student Services: I was too shy to ask for the things I could get help with. When I went back as an adult student, I got my papers read for better grades. They helped me with employment. University is a little community. Unless you seek help, it won't come to you. The bottom line is, you must actively search for your needs. Don't be afraid to ask for help, because if you don't, you will be in trouble!

LAURA HERAUF, B.Ed., **University of Regina**

Don't follow your high school sweetheart to college. That's a bad reason to choose a college. Live in the dorm the first year. Then you get exposed to more people. Then you grow your friend base. Don't wear women's clothes, because then your brother will take a picture of you and show your parents.

PHIL HILGER, B.S. Mechanical Engineering Technology, **Purdue University**

Drink less. Study more.

BILL SLIGER, B.S. Engineering Technology

You have to learn balance. Balance between school work and a social life. You can't just party and forget about school. But you can't just be immersed in school either!

MELANIE DELA CRUZ, currently a French Major

What I wish I knew then... that studying at university can be exhausting! Being at a computer desk and reading makes you physically tired. Your body needs to be stretched so that your mind can function. If you do not stretch, you get stiff and tired, and become less able to deal with the required readings and paper writing. Taking time to stretch regularly really gets your blood circulating and gives your body a chance to de-stress from the mental exercise it has been performing. Pilates, yoga and gymnastics have helped me to get through university and continue to assist me in dealing with the continued desk demands of my career.

ANNA BOGAR, B.A., LL.B., **University of Saskatchewan**

My advice would be to learn how to communicate with other people and learn how to ask for help. Otherwise you feel isolated and you will not like where you are. Any time you begin to feel isolated, you will not want to continue studying at your institution.

JEAN L. DEHART
Ph.D Communications, **University of Georgia**
M.S. Communications, **University of Tennessee**
B.S. Political Communications, **James Madison University**

Each individual person has to ask themselves what kind of social life they want. A school cannot teach you how to make friends. College cannot teach you "how not to be a social reject"—you have to get out of your apartment and talk to other students to make friends. These skills you should have learned in elementary school class; turn around and say hello!

SHELLY POCHA, College Diploma in Special Needs Education, **Canadian University College**

Study hard and play hard. If you do not go out and socialize you will burn out. My fourth year student mentor that I was assigned to told me to socialize, otherwise you will be exhausted. I wish I had fallen asleep less in class. They did not teach us enough business management in Veterinarian Medicine.

CYNTHIA STOCK, B.A. Agriculture, Ph.D Veterinary Medicine

Share your crayons! I went to university for six years and not once did anyone share their crayons in my design classes. They came and they went day in and day out, not talking to each other and not sharing their art tools. They studied for themselves and kept their art work singular. What an absolute shame, we could have learned to share much more than those crayons. We could have learned to share ideas that would one day alter societies' environment for the better.

GARY CHRISTOPHER, BSc Environmental Design
Finishing M.S. Environmental Design, **University of Manitoba**

Don't eat yellow snow!

TRINA, RNA Diploma, **Kelsey Campus, SIAST**

Be who you are. Be real; one of the things I noticed about aboriginal people going to cities to take college classes is they tried to assimilate. By assimilating into the white culture too much, they lost their culture. This hurt them because they lost who they were. Most universities and colleges have a culture in and of itself, so if you are not comfortable with whom you are, you will be too scared to fully participate and engage in group discussions. If you are comfortable with whom you are, you can learn from others and hear other philosophies without being threatened.

GLORIA LETENDRE, BSc Nursing,
current Master's student, **University of Alberta**

University changed me big time. University really gives you an opportunity to define who you are. It was a good transitional experience of leaving home and learning how much you can handle. I left a child and became a woman. The experience stretched me and helped me grow. I was a "homebody", so I was forced to get to know people and navigate opportunities. I had to go outside of myself. I got to know myself, and It changed me. Many of my classmates' personalities changed in a good way.

ANGELA QIODRADU, B.A., B.Ed., **University of Lethbridge**

University doesn't do a good job of making a nontraditional student feel at home. Considering the diverse population here in my city, the diversity here on campus is disheartening. The amount of people whom I can identify/relate to is minimal, at best.

JASON, B.A. English Writing Concentration, **Indiana University**

If you live close to the university you attend, do not go home every weekend, because you miss out on developing relationships with other people in your dorm. Try dorm life, because you'll meet people that are different than you, and as we all know, when you grow up, you're around people who are the same as you. My first two years, there were 3 guys from Kenya and 1 from Nigeria. We ended up playing rugby together. It was through freshman orientation that I helped lead that I became good friends with a guy from Canada.

JEREMY BROOK, BSc Nursing, **Cornerstone University**
A.D.N. **Grand Rapids Community College**

Take your time getting involved in a relationship. We were dating for a few months, and people kept looking for a ring on my left finger. We didn't want to get married until we graduated.

JULIA KLUSMAN, B.S. Marketing, **Franciscan University of Steubenville**

When I was going, I dropped out of high school, returned for my GED, and ten years later, got a job at a daycare. I didn't think I was smart enough to take classes, but I did, and it really makes me feel good about myself.

LINDA DAVIS, B.A. Psychology, **University of Sacred Heart and St. Joseph's College**

Remain focused, keeping in sight your longer term career goals, but maintain a balance between pursuance of your academic endeavors and participating in the abundance of student activities on campus; and recognize the excellent student support systems available and utilize them if needed, as they exist for you.

DAVID HARRIS, BSc Physics, MBA, **University of Saskatchewan**

It was more fun to meet new friends than the actual studying. The social aspect of college was great!!

JENN SUEDE, Food & Nutrition Management, **Kelsey Campus, SIAST**

If spending time with your friends is getting in the way of your studying, study with them. Study groups are a good time. They're also a saviour if you didn't read the book or missed too many lectures. A word to 1st-year artsy students: don't play your guitar and sing close to residence windows past 10 pm. Waking up a 4th-year-exhausted-interning student can be scary. Plan your schedule carefully. School was easy for me; I crammed at the last minute and spent most of my time investing in friendships.

Make a point of chilling with a friend on a daily basis. When you graduate, your jobs will change, but you'll always have the friends with whom you invested your time.

MARY HEIER, B.A. English Lit., minor in French and Education, **Franciscan University of Steubenville**

Don't live with someone you went to high school with. You miss out on an opportunity to meet great people. Your best friend isn't necessarily the best person to live with. Sometimes a little separation is good. I've known people who have ruined great friendships because they decided to room together.

CRAIG SHANNON, B.S., M.P.T. Physical Therapy, **Central Michigan and University of Michigan**

If you are in a large college or university don't go to orientation expecting to make lifelong friends. Friends will pop up in unexpected places.

ASHLY NORDBY, currently studying at university (un-declared major)

Lonely people say and do mean things. Nice people say and do nice things.

CARMON HAMPTON, RN Diploma

$$\Rightarrow \sin x \tan x$$

$$\Rightarrow \sin x \left(\sin x / \cos \right.$$

$$\Rightarrow \sin^2 x / \cos x =$$

$$\Rightarrow \sin^2 x / \cos x = ($$

$$\Rightarrow \underline{\sin^2 x}$$

CHAPTER FOUR

College did not teach us to learn

No Pain, No Brain!

As I was resting on a musty futon and snuggled under my grandma's violet quilt, rays of sunlight were peeping through the blinds, dancing sweetly on my fatigued eyelids. My energetic roommate had left my door ajar, in the hopes that I would awaken willingly to the noises of her preparation. I lay still blinking profusely in the hopes that I would whisk away wrinkles caused by sleep deprivation. My best friend was taking me to an early morning class at our excellence-driven university, which religiously enforced a dress code. She weakened my resistance daily by brewing specialty coffee and allowing the aroma to awake my senses. She was a disciplined young woman with a work ethic that I could not comprehend. She had already been awake for two hours that morning to study, and could not fathom that I would entertain the wayward thought of skipping my Creative Writing class. She was a Biology major who believed in not only attending class, but being on time. She would ritually stand by the apartment entrance, holding a travel mug of fresh coffee with delightful flavor to lure me out of the warm apartment and into the car. I mumbled to her each morning that the Biology professors should study students who believed in attending classes on time, because they were creating a paradigm shift within the academic community. Until that semester, I had naturally assumed that the subtleties of my humour were enjoyed by more than just my Political Science classmates.

I kept reminding her, as I quickly threw on my jean skirt and black t-shirt, that I was independent. While I brushed my teeth and pulled my long thick rusty brown hair in an elastic tie, searching frantically for my flip flops, I reminded her that my friends and I were political activists and artisans that did *not* wake up at six in the morning to achieve 'higher learning'. I was also trying to avoid returning to my first upper level Public Administration class that I had optimistically enrolled in. After the first class, I had an eerie sense that it would require *EFFORT* and was devastated by the weight of my textbook. In my naïveté, I supposed that senior political science classes would be a quiet little meeting hosted by intelligentsia. Instead, we had jaded professors from western states telling us the deficit would never be reduced, and therefore we should consider leading a revolution. We were the children of the hippies—willing social activists and reformers—passionate, aggressive, and willing to die for what we believed in... as long as "the cause" started after lunch.

The media refers to my age group as 'Generation X': the lost generation. As I reminded my roommate of our political struggles, we shuffled down the apartment hallway towards her car. Due to her training in the scientific field, she possessed a high level of patience. By the time we had reached the car, I had already informed her of my visit to the Congress building in the United States, where I discussed socio-economic policies with a Senator.

In short, I was explaining to her that we were undisciplined flower children, who vaguely believed in prayer or philosophy; God's will was mystical and not attainable; and logic was sought, but rarely achieved. I was trying to convince her that Socrates himself would not support an early morning philosophy class. Political Studies majors only believed in **coffee**. It was the only thing we could almost agree on, if we did not discuss propaganda, fair trade policies, and nutritional content. College was merely a place that we were going to impact with our radical ideas, not to be changed by scholastic routine. We had not matured enough to recognize that true knowledge and understanding are sought by the wise. Academic excellence is achieved by being balanced, discovery, creating a disciplined lifestyle, and by embracing a journey of 'life-learning'.

The college campus is a very exciting place, with stimulating debates provoked by philosophical types. Many of my friends and I were not only artistic social butterflies, but we also had a hunger for learning. That is why we committed the most unpardonable sin that all freshmen seem to do: *seeking knowledge rabidly like a starving dog!* The abrupt processing of information caused us an exhilarating sensation we were not accustomed to, leading us into our first experience with **burnout.** College is not only mentally and visually stimulating, but also emotionally and socially invigorating, which creates a long lasting euphoric high, right up until Thanksgiving.

Thanksgiving was the holiday where students sat fidgeting impatiently in the car, because we could hardly wait to get home and tell our parents how bright we were. We could not enjoy the long drive home, because we needed to explain to our mothers what we learned, show them our new textbooks and gossip about our roommate's mental fixation with polishing kitchen utensils. What really happens?? Once a student falls into their mother's arms there is a flood of tears from over-exhaustion, and a need to sleep for the next 27 hours. This leaves Mom with the impression that her child is having a nervous breakdown as a result of the coffee and six sandwiches she just saw her child consume, and the bowl of mint-chocolate -chip ice cream that only graduates can afford.

The reason for this exhaustion is simply due to too much stress at one time. Freshman need to realize that the first semester is an adjustment period, and the most valuable lesson they can learn from that period is to achieve balance. **Balance is the ability to set priorities.** Often young people are so enamoured by the experience of 'instant freedom' that they do not establish new priorities for their college experience. In high school, students are taught to manage one class at a time, while college forces a student to multi-task. It is up to the student to define for themselves what they want to realistically achieve in college, and what is most important to them. This is why it is wisdom to reassess your priorities daily. I observed in dorms how some of my friends would either study all the time including weekends, while other friends would sit in the halls goofing off with their new friends.

College can last anywhere from two years to eight years, depending on the courses and what level of education students want to achieve. Although it does indeed go by very fast, it can also consume a young person's mind like the speed of a twisting tornado. If a college student is sucked up into the eye of the storm, it may seem calm for awhile... until they are spit out and flung into some random field where they are left feeling abandoned.

"Balance" is achieving what is expected,
without compromising what is necessary.

Setting priorities will be an anchor for a student overwhelmed by the many demands of college life. In the real world, employees are expected to drop everything for an emergency in their work environment. **Only those who**

have learned the art of flexibility will advance in their careers as successful problem solvers. Determine how to make the best use of your time, while maintaining the core values that anchor your life. By carefully planning your schedule, time and thoughts, you will easily adapt to your environment and the people you need to understand.

Learning about the people around you is just as important as reading your text books. One day you will eventually be working with a team. A wise boss will hire different personalities in order to have a well rounded team. It will be imperative to understand how others facilitate and communicate. Dorms are an excellent opportunity to differentiate personality types, and how to get along with them. Living with a roommate in college is also an excellent self awareness experience. Until you have a room mate in college you will not realize that you have numerous character flaws that need improving.

Hint: *If you cannot let your roommate 'touch' your day planner because she is supposedly an 'untreatable artist with the attention span of a cat' and your entire life is in that book, it is time to cut back on the java, and go to a movie with your roommate. In case your eyes have just glossed over, I am nicely telling you that you are a 'TYPE A' PERSONALITY WITH CONTROL ISSUES.*

It is alright; you will live, conquer, and prove to all the personality-types that you will achieve more than everyone else! However, on the odd chance that it drives you to narcotics, makes you friendless, and your nickname at work is "cut throat"—you might want to learn while you are still young to RELAX!!!

I must warn you about the "overachieving oldest child" that may share your dorm room or apartment. If your roommate tells you that they prefer to be in bed with ABSOLUTE SILENCE by 10 pm to help them focus in class the next morning, earnestly run down the hallway in your boxers screaming, "Eldest child, going to bed! She's going to bed! Silence, everyone!!!" The reason for this is that if you make the overachieving roommate angry, you will suffer an enduring wrath that you did not think was possible.

The eldest children in most families are diabolical strategists, and will not hesitate to offer you money to go out for pizza. The reason they send you away from the apartment is so that they are home that evening to answer the phone when your mother calls. They will befriend her, talk with her for thirty minutes and suggest that if you had less pizza money you might take your studying a little more seriously, and perhaps it would be best to have an 'intervention' meeting over Christmas. She will also ask to speak to your father, making him realize that he likes her better than you, to convince him that you really do need to wear those 1980s dollar-store glasses that he bought you—and stop being so vain!

I will never forget when my roommate came home with my mother after a day of shopping. I could not find them, and I was sitting in the kitchen frantically calling every store or hospital I could think of. They both walked in smiling with absolute delight and girlish abandonment, and pointed to the new shoes that my mother bought her for putting up with me. Someone else's oldest child got new shoes from my mother when it was not even a holiday!

A dark fear came over me like impending doom, as I quickly surmised that the political dynamics of our friendship and 'room sharing' had changed. The rules have never been the same since—and I will always pinpoint it to that one foolish night I thought she would enjoy having some of my friends over for pizza and wings. Your serious roommate will like this idea about as much as they want their mother to reproduce more children. They DON'T, and they never will... always warn your friends about your roommate before you invite them over. NEVER MESS WITH THE OVER-ACHIEVING ELDEST CHILD!!!

So before you decide with your friends that the "serious girl" in the dorm needs to be pranked to help her relax, you might want to evaluate whether she will think it's funny to return to her room only to find her bed mattress missing. She might not enjoy looking at a little feminine napkin with a note stating that "I tried to wash the mattress for you, but it shrunk".

Hint: *If she is strong and capable of moving you off the bed, flinging your quilt on the floor, and then willing to sleep in your bed while reminding you that there WILL be a phone call made to your mother early Sunday morning before church starts, you might want to follow my advice.*

All of us younger members in the family know it is funny, but you are going to take a risk! It may be wise to take some precautions when you're planning a diabolical scheme involving your roommate.

CONSIDER THESE SAFETY TIPS FOR ANY PRANK:

1. MAKE SURE THAT YOU DO NOT SLEEP IN THE SAME ROOM the night that they come home. It's never wise to be around when the poop hits the fan.

2. MAKE SURE YOU HAVE THE PHONE DISCONNECTED for a solid 72 hours. If you tell them you forgot to pay the phone bill, you are a "Type B" personality... they WILL believe you.

3. Always do it within 48 hours of a church service—they are guilt ridden because of Mom, and will spend Sunday morning asking God to forgive them for anger. They will also pray for strength to endure you, because they instinctively know that you are the result of answered prayers by their younger sister.

4. REMEMBER THAT YOUR ROOMMATE IS PROBABLY SMARTER THAN YOU (the very reason they have a cumulative GPA of 3.8), and there WILL be a embarrassing payback!

5. If they are an overachieving oldest child in the family: ABORT THE MISSION!!!! ABORT THE MISSION!!!

Pranks may prevent you in the future from being an effective team player—but sometimes they are just plain college fun.

Another reason for failing to be a good team player could be self-imposed isolation. You will have future co-workers who not only have a completely different set of values than you, but they will not think like you. You must learn to appreciate others and speak their language, developing the skill of observation. Watch how your friends and roommates in college organize their desks. Do they lend their CDs, books, and personal property, or do they prefer not to? Where do they put their school bag, and how do they study? Do your roommates keep track of birthdays, or remember appointments on your behalf? These simple observations will teach you to pay attention to your future co-workers. In order to work peaceably with others, you must learn how others work. College is a wonderful array of diverse cultures with surprising opportunities to socialize and learn. If a student is organized with his or her time and priorities, he or she will be able to uncover and enjoy the complex beauty of people.

Organization is the key to surviving deadlines, demands and the social dynamics in college. Before leaving home for each semester of university, write a list! The first thing on your practical list should be the DETAILS of what needs to be done before you leave for college. If you are leaving home to live in another state or country, you must have all of your paperwork in order to obtain a travel visa at least two months before you leave. Then you  will have time to make adjustments in case anything goes awry. In this day and age with all the changes in the international community, it would be wisdom for North American students going to college in the United States or Canada to travel with a passport instead of a birth certificate. Guard your passport with your life. Do not give it to your laid-back roommate to hold on to!!

Once you are accepted into college and have decided to definitely attend that college, check out their website. Find a list of phone numbers and contacts that you might possibly need, and write them down in the new day planner you just bought from Stuff-Mart. Look on the college website for a list of advisors, the phone numbers for the finance office, the student loan department, the administration office, the library, and the student housing administrator. YOUR STUDENT LOAN NEEDS TO BE FILLED OUT AND SENT AWAY EIGHT WEEKS BEFORE CLASS STARTS. You can also check their website for the classes that you enroled in (*YES*—enrol ahead of time before the wave of students hits). Find out what classes and which room numbers you will be attending. Look on the website for a campus map to memorize your new surroundings, and PAY FOR PARKING AS SOON AS YOU ARE ALLOWED TO BUY PARKING. Have your parents pay for it before they discover how much they will be paying for everything else! It is referred to as "stealth planning".

Knowing what and when to call Dad for money is also very important to surviving your freshman year with your sanity intact. The first lesson you want to learn with Dad is that he loves to hear the words "I am ORGANIZED". If you are not the first kid in the family going to college, it will be very difficult to convince him that parking costs twice as much as it really does (so you have extra money for pizza). You will therefore need an alternate plan and must learn the college lingo in order to convince Dad of anything!! By the second child, Dad has learned to quickly ask you to show him your list of bills. If you are the fourth child to go to college (like me), do not think you will ever taste a piece of pie from the expensive cafeteria unless you are street smart!!

Hint: *If you are the youngest child in the family going to college and you need more money from Dad, you will need to show him a day planner, mission statement, financial budget projections, spreadsheet, and 10-point proposal on why you are much more responsible than other college students who obviously have a higher debt equity ratio. Be sure to include a return on assets ratio with a possible interest recovery payback period. These financial statements are the only thing that will win Dad over! Do not use fancy semigloss cover either, or he will know that you can afford it.*

Do not get me wrong—Mom is an integral part of your success in college; however you want to pace yourself with Mom. Remember that Mom is a buffer between you and Dad, when you have to explain that you failed Calculus and your financial projections were "off"—give or take a couple of hundred dollars. You will also need Mom for other organizational reasons. Mothers will help you write a paper in a crunch! Her soft heart and inability to fathom that you could possibly fail, will make her engage in tasks you did not think possible. For example, she will call up that sweet southern friend that she knows who has a cute son with broad shoulders, beautiful blue eyes and a 3.8 GPA, that took exactly the class you are struggling with. If he is willing to tutor you for free, and help you write that essay in the next 24 hours, she has agreed to bake him a lemon meringue pie two inches high.

Never de-value "Mom connections"; when you are 21, you will realize the woman is a GENIUS!! You will appreciate her problem-solving skills if you have gone through counseling and learned to pray through the angst you have. This angst is due to Mom consistently embarrassing you in front of your friend as payback for giving away your "Christmas sweater". Once again, your roommate parades around in your parents' house with the ugly sweater that Mom sent you—after you begged her never to wear it again. Learn to forgive Mom, or choose wiser friends who are in tune with the social dynamics of your dysfunctional family structure!

> ### Survival Tip #10:
>
> *College will not teach you or enforce you to be disciplined. You will have to be your own enforcer.*

One of the classic mistakes that freshmen usually make is that they don't value learning the discipline that they will need to succeed. When a professor gives you 30 days to complete an essay, it may be fantastically shocking in your first year to find out that they think you will actually use those 30 days to research, prepare, organize and write the essay. Why on earth would any student start writing, researching, and cutting and pasting information from the Internet the night before it is due?! WHO WOULD DO SUCH A THING??? If you fail at your dreams, it is usually because you were lazy, unprepared, and/or handled your finances improperly. It is imperative in your first year that you teach yourself to be disciplined.

The first day of your essay assignment, write down an outline to guide your research; i.e. if you have 30 days to complete it, plan to do at least one hour of research each day for the next two weeks. Then spend the following week writing, and allow time for editing and designing your organized layout. In the first week, buy a package of colored recipe cards. Write each of your main arguments on a different coloured card. Then for each argument or point that you want to prove, write a footnote on that coloured card.

For example, if you are trying to prove that cowboys are hot, write *"Point #1"* on a green card: *They are hot because they work with their hands.* Then, on all the other green cards, write quotes with the evidence you've found proving why strong hands are essential.

Hint: *Write the bibliography information on the same card as your quote. That way, when you are trying to finish your bibliography at 5:00 a.m. to meet the essay deadline for 7:00 a.m., you can quickly finish without looking frantically for information.*

This is a far-fetched, post-modern idea; however, you could try to get the essay done EARLY. Yeah, I almost laughed out loud while writing that thought!! Make sure you are disciplined in recording your research findings. If you are studying languages, write your verbs out on those recipe cards and use them as flash cards every night before bed. When I started doing that, I was able to increase my average by 26%. In college it's very difficult to bring up an average by that much, so fast. Recipe cards that cost all of a few dollars will be worth every penny!

Always remind yourself while you study and complete assignments that your professor is *not* responsible for your success. Your professor is not the one to be writing your paper, so take advantage of his advice *before* it is due. Show your professor that you are capable of doing your own research. If you are struggling with academic writing, attend an essay-writing workshop and learn how to express yourself properly in formal writing. Every college offers writing workshops. Invest in whatever you need to succeed!

> *If you do not ask for help when you know you need it, that is laziness—not failure.*

If you are a hard-working, proactive student, you will take responsibility for completing core requirements. It is also your responsibility to understand deadlines of an administrative nature. If you make an appointment with a financial advisor—keep it!! Do not think that you can skip it to go for lunch with your friends, and simply arrange a new one. Those habits will indeed follow you into your internship and any job that follows. Learn in your first year to keep appointments, and call ahead to confirm it. Your professor will definitely remember who you are (in a bad way) if you made him or her travel all the way back to the campus, only to find out that you were a "no show".

I personally found this aspect of college very difficult. Being a social butterfly, I did not own a watch, and I thought day planners were last minute options for taking notes in the couple of early morning classes that I actually attended. I took this poor habit with me into my adult career, causing damaging repercussions to my reputation. It is difficult for professionals to respect young adults who don't honour appointments. It implies that you don't really care about their input or their time. You should mark the deadline dates on your calendar, because they really are deadline dates (*Fees for missing deadlines will cost more than your food budget for the month! If you have to share food with your cat, Friskies is the way to go*).

Another common reason for failure in college is simply a lack of planning. In this era of Internet access, find a map of your new location and memorize important buildings *before* you get there! Find out where the emergency centers are, and have a strategy in place of what to do in the event of a crisis. When in shock, it is very difficult to think logically during serious trauma. An emergency occurs when least expected, and sometimes may be the result of poorly thought-out decisions.

I remember being so financially tight in my second semester when my best friend and I decided to move into our own apartment that we did everything that we could to cut costs. In the living room, we had two chairs and a television. In the bedrooms were desks, my old rickety computer displaying my high score in Tetris, and our beds, which consisted of mattresses on the floor with homemade quilts that our grandmothers had made. It doesn't matter what you have to endure financially when you have the quilt that your grandma made wrapped around you.

There was no money even for an economy oil change for my trusty hatchback, so we decided to do it ourselves. My roommate was experienced in this area, so we were confident in her ability to find an abandoned parking lot for this purpose. Something went horribly wrong while she was working under the car, and the "safeties" buckled. As a result, I watched my car collapse on my best friend with a loud thump. Nothing seizes your heart like watching a best friend or a loved one endure an accident. My heart pulsated, and my arms experienced numbness. I have never felt so helpless in my life. Then I heard her scream with absolute angst in her voice—the large hot engine had landed on her shoulder and back, burning her flesh deeper with each passing second. I tried to lift the car but I couldn't; it was just too heavy.

She knew, even in the middle of absolute panic, that the only way to rescue her was for me to get in the car and drive backwards—risking her death. It was a desperate solution, for a desperate situation. It was a rare experience where I tangibly felt the presence of an angel. As I drove backwards over her I screamed loudly, "Please God, don't let me be the one to murder my best friend!!", and then I literally felt the car lift up a foot high as I put the car in reverse. I thought it was because I was driving over my best friend's head... but later we both realized an angel was present. She saw the car lift into the air, long enough for her to be able to roll out from under the car. We rushed home and I immediately phoned my mother, who is a nurse practitioner, for help. Without current first-aid knowledge, we didn't grasp that she sustained third degree burns—because she could not feel any pain.

Thank the good Lord in heaven my mother takes my calls when she is working. She stopped everything to talk us through the crisis. This is an unforgettable experience in which I learned the important of making plans in case of an emergency.

What will YOU do if something happens at university? Do you have parents that will answer the phone and help you in time of trouble? If not, you need a list of phone numbers on your fridge in case of an emergency. You will not be thinking clearly when you are panicked. You also need emergency contact numbers on your fridge in case someone has to break into your apartment to find you.

As a result of the accident, we were faced with our own mortality at a young age. The fragility of humanity is not to be forgotten. After that tramatic event, we had such a difficult time focusing on our college assignments. My average dropped by 10 percent, and I just couldn't seem to shake off the panic and stress that I felt every night. Unfortunately, university culture does not allow for much mercy in a time of personal trauma. They may defer an exam, but they will not automatically offer you the help that you need. If you have experienced a traumatic event, proactively seek out a counselor—it will help you to know that you are not alone. There is always free counseling available at a church. If you are hesitant to seek out spiritual counsel, at least consult with a health professional on campus for a referral.

Most psychologists will tell you to never make any sudden or important decisions after a trauma such as this. If you have been in an accident, lost a loved one or experienced a major trauma, do not make any decisions about college. Give yourself a couple of months to recover, and allow yourself to heal properly. Keep focused on finishing your course material, studying for finals, and coping with the daily emotions that  surface. It is very difficult to cope with a person's death while concentrating on a final exam. There is no shame in asking if you qualify for an exam deferral. It is your responsibility to go to the department's office and ask for the form. Often they will ask you to provide an official note of some kind.

When my grandmother passed away the night of my final exam, I was completely devastated. She was a children's author, my "anchor", and mentor. I had just lost the one person who believed in me the most. Even though I had a loving and supportive mother, a special bond with a caring grandparent is unique and irreplaceable. I asked a good friend of mine to come over to my apartment every morning for a week—just to help me with my daily routine, so that I would not lie in bed in a daze, feeling lost and alone. It was very difficult to keep functioning; however I had to, in order to finish my semester.

> ### Survival Tip #11:
>
> *College will not help you focus, operating at the fast pace that it does, regardless of what personal trauma you may be dealing with.*

When you cannot sleep properly and are experiencing nightmares, drink something warm, listen to some soft music, review your life, and remind yourself what you are thankful to God for. Lack of sleep sometimes comes from replaying those stressful scenarios in your mind. While you lay in bed, use the same thought process to replay good scenarios; envision your new future, and think of new interesting goals that you are going to make. Visualize yourself succeeding, being happy, and seeing your dreams come true. I often read from the Psalms in the Bible, so that my soul would be at rest. I found the Psalms to be very calming. I prayed before bedtime and asked Jesus to calm my mind.

Forgiving and releasing anger before sleeping also helps the body to rest peacefully. Anger is a powerful negative force that pulses through your veins like poison. That is why the Psalms warn against going to bed with anger or unforgiveness in your heart. It is easier to sleep and function when you are at peace with yourself and others. It is easier to face a new day with a smile and hope. Hope creates a positive force in your life, bringing joy and laughter to your daily routine. It has also been proven medically that people who laugh more often are healthier.

List those positive long range scholastic goals in your journal that you want to achieve. College will not teach you to learn and focus during difficult times in your life. It takes a mature decision to frame your world with a positive outlook. Regardless of what you are facing while attending college, you must spend approximately three productive hours learning on your own for every hour of class time. Therefore, it is up to you to discipline your mind to focus on what you are learning in class, whether you are tired and stressed or not. Let me assure you—when a professor talks like Homer Simpson and the course material is very dry, it will be difficult not to dream of your favourite sweet breakfast cereal and the final episode of a dramatic TV series. I remember counting every single roof tile in my Governmental Public Policy class.

Looking over your vision can sometimes help you focus on school, rather than question why the roof tiles have grungy stains on every second one.

Write in your journal some goals that you want to achieve each semester, and how you are going to achieve them. I have scored 100% on many exams and class assignments; unfortunately, I have also received 30% in some mathematic midterms. (Statistics classes were created by Lucifer!) Make a mental list each day of the chapters you are going to review, and how much time you will devote to each subject. Use your microwave timer if you have to, timing how long you will allow yourself to watch television. DO NOT GET INTO THE HABIT OF STUDYING IN FRONT OF THE TV!!! It will only distract you.

The common thread in classes I failed was personal absence, a strong dislike for my professor, and my inability to focus on the material. Each of these three issues will waste valuable study time. If you skip classes, you will need twice the time to study because of learning what you missed in class, and spending time pursuing classmates' notes. If you dislike a professor, you will often waste time arguing, ignoring important information, and even disputing grades. If you are unable to focus on the material, you will lose time catching up before the final, or retaking the failed class. **This is why it is basic wisdom to protect your time, and your mind.**

Attend your labs at all cost. There are teachers' aids there—much cheaper than a tutor! Hire a tutor when you are not grasping the material or when your marks reach anything lower than a 70%. Do not phone a tutor to ask for help three days before a final. **Hint:** *Be realistic; they can only help you help yourself.* The best tutors are very busy and are just as popular as successful golf players. Book three weeks in advance, and put aside what you owe them from each paycheque. The quickest way to lose a tutor is to argue over money owed. Treat them right—they are saving your behind!

Another time-wasting pit I saw other students fall into was the constant switching of major and minor fields of study in the middle of a term. One semester they were English majors; the next semester they were Biology majors. This type of illogical shift will only result in lower grades and confusion. If you are really miserable, consider changing your major. However, change it *only* after seeking the advice of a counselor, your parents, and the professors—relative to your new field of study. Check with seniors who are trying to graduate in that field, who have a long and distinguished list of trials they wished they had avoided. Don't make rash decisions just because you received a low grade on your last quiz... or because you think your math professor looks like a geek and really needs to take a bath. Trust me; the temptation will arise with some professors!

Life is about getting up after you fall. The winner is not the person who never fell; the winner is the person who once again rises to their feet. Learn to recover quickly from mistakes, and avoid making emotional decisions that will jeopardize your major. Learn to appreciate the information offered to you in class without needing to qualify your opinions. Course material studied in your major is merely laying a foundation for your future career. Therefore it is imperative to separate factual decisions from impulsive ones.

When I was a young Political Science major, I thought that every piece of information was important, and deeply pondered on everything taught to me. I thought everyone who was *educated* was *smart*. That was, until I saw them stumbling home drunk because they couldn't find their car keys.

Deeply dwelling on every fact you research can become an inefficient use of your time—especially when you have convinced yourself that your thinking time was more important than writing the essay. JUST WRITE THE ESSAY, OH DEEP BRILLIANT ONE... tweak later. When you are attending university, learn quickly what needs to be thought through, and which details need only to be memorized. If you are not successful in discerning the difference within your first few classes, talk to your professors and ask them if you absorbed the class material that they feel is most important. As you progress, you will use your time more efficiently to fulfill your calling in life. It would be a shame to wake up at age 30 and realize that six of those years were wasted being distracted from your scholastic dream.

Whether parents realize this or not, a lot of money is lost while attending college due to faulty planning and lack of vision. Having realistic goals will save students hundreds of dollars. For example, withdrawing from three classes that proved to be too difficult for you, will result in a $1000 loss. Failing to make payments or hand in correct paperwork will cost a minimum of $500. Failing to pay rent or utility bills on time will cost $300 extra in NSF charges and or credit card interest. Failing to use the house phone with your friends and using your cell phone instead may cost a student an extra $2000 during the academic year (depending on the woman: we all instinctively know that men only call when they are in love or need money). Eating out because you did not have time to cook, or the sudden realization that you're hungry before your three hour evening class, could cost you an extra $100 per week. Lastly, but very important, is the reality that driving a car, getting parking tickets and speeding tickets might add up to an extra $1000 that year. It may be wisdom to consider getting a bus pass, even if you do own a car! The bottom line in all of this is that unexpected financial waste increases stress, and will have an astonishing negative impact on a student's overall scholastic performance and their family relationships. PLAN AHEAD, GET ORGANIZED AND BE REALISTIC!!

10 PLACES TO AVOID STUDYING WHEN YOU ARE PREPARING FOR A FINAL EXAM:

10. GRANDMA'S PLACE; she is cute, old, and she will feed you. You will become weak, help her dust, and listen to her stories. Tell her you love her, and that is why you are going to visit AFTER your exam.

9. DO NOT STUDY IN THE HOSPITAL EMERGENCY ROOM, all because you were dancing in your socks as a stress release in the carpeted living room when you fell on your glass of juice, cutting your wrist open. Trust me—if it weren't for the drunk cowboys in the next room who flew off the back of their truck from 'tail surfing' at 30 miles an hour, requiring over 50 stitches—I would have spent the entire evening with a psychiatrist, trying to assure her that I am *not* "one of those" suicidal students, and that the four stitches were legitimately needed. Eventually the attending doctor unstrapped my arm from the bed and released me to go home. Remember: if the truth about what happened sounds more retarded than what they *think* happened, keep quiet... it will get you free jello!

8. APPARENTLY, THE REALLY SMART PEOPLE can watch television, talk on the phone, and have their favorite song playing while studying. Hmmm... sounds fishy to me... go study in the library!

7. UMMM, NO, THE BAR IS NOT A STUDY HALL unless you are studying for Women and Gender Studies, or Economics. The experience may give you insightful analogies.

6. If your boyfriend is a hottie with big beautiful eyes, or your conniving girlfriend is offering to pay for your supper and an action movie FOR THE FIRST TIME, avoid them like the plague during final exams!!!

5. NEVER STUDY AT DAD'S HOUSE. He will spend three hours teaching you how to study. This could make you rethink marriage, your life, and all of the injustices in society—all in one short evening.

4. BELIEVE IT OR NOT, THE LOCAL CONVENIENCE STORE is not a study hall either. So you really do need the slushie... now get back to work!!

3. YEAH, I THOUGHT THAT FUNKY CAFÉ would help me to relax too. Until I got into the music, bumped into my friends, and enjoyed a cookie or two... alright, maybe four... and ended up in a hostile philosophical debate with the Sociology majors about the "cultural suppressions of American marketing and how propaganda influences our socio-economic decisions". I know, it sounds like smack to me too, but apparently it came in handy on my economics exam... (and hey... what were they doing drinking coffee... shouldn't they be drinking something organic??)

2. NOPE, THE CHEAPY THEATRE is not helping you pass your American History midterm in the morning—and don't think that if you are a Political Science major, watching *Black Hawk Down* will prepare you for the Foreign Policy exam. Movies are not a replacement for actually reading the textbook. Trust me... writing that President Lincoln's assassination was 'subjective' on my essay, because I couldn't remember which president he was, really back fired on me. (Oh yeah—do not suggest that Cromwell was a fascist, either!)

1. LAYING ON YOUR BED while you practise Spanish verbs or study French poetry: wrong place on so many levels.

The reason students often cram for exams and try to merely regurgitate information is because they have not embraced the journey of life-learning. They often come directly from high school, wanting information to be spoon-fed to them. Wise students ascertain that true knowledge and understanding comes from consistently seeking. Always maintain a childlike curiosity; constantly exploring, investigating and watching.

Take at least one class every semester that is new and enjoyable, rather than only what is within your comfort zone. If you are an Education major, try taking a language that semester. You may find out that you really enjoy Spanish, and teach in a Spanish country for a year.

It is much easier to try something new when you are already focused and know which major you will be taking for the next four years. When you know what you are called by God to do with your life, and what you are truly passionate about, it is much easier to experiment and challenge yourself without becoming frightened. If you are a college student who is fearful all the time, you are not aware of your calling or what you are passionate about!! **Passion, according to the dictionary, is any powerful or compelling emotion or feeling.** If you envision yourself learning for the rest of your life, you will seek courses that stimulate you. You will make choices that help you feel alive, enforcing that the dreams you have are real.

When each day counts, and your priorities are protected by the decisions you make, you will begin the journey of life-learning. Pay attention to what is going on around you, widening your focus. Professionals who respect their field continue to read, and are proactive in their learning. Attend courses that challenge you, and be involved in your community. Variety is often a catalyst for excitement. Do not waste money with all of your class withdrawals purely because you were a dreamer, and thought that you could handle Finance 101 as your elective. If you are already struggling with the classes that are in your major, do not choose an elective that is even more difficult and discouraging. Use it as an opportunity to take a class you will really enjoy.

> ### *Life-learners are selective in their learning, and have discovered what is stealing their time.*

Becoming a life-learner starts with a desire and passion for the journey of discovery. Enjoying the journey comes from understanding how to balance your priorities. Disorder is the result of sacrificing priorities. Reducing costs cannot interfere with protecting valuable time. Having a social life cannot be at the expense of studying. Balancing all of these diverse dynamics will initiate peace in your life, and reduce the pressures of deadlines.

Having a balanced life in college will make your scholastic and career path more productive. When priorities are protected because a student's schedule and finances are organized, it is much easier to enjoy life and all that it has to offer.

Since this human need for balance is vital, it is imperative to develop and maintain a disciplined lifestyle while working with a variety of people. Not all people that you associate with or try to help will have the same priorities as you. Not all of the people in your sphere of influence will achieve goals at the same pace as you. It will take maturity to learn how to flow with others, because they are on their own journey of life-learning. This disciplined lifestyle requires a mutual respect for each other, and a great amount of bravery to accept that life-learning may take all of you in different directions.

It requires bravery to conquer any student's greatest enemy: procrastination. Fear of failure is why students will avoid progressing in college. A fulfilling learning experience comes from making "now" decisions. *NOW* is always the time—not tomorrow. When you daily achieve your smaller goals in college, it builds confidence towards achieving the larger goal. The ultimate goal in college is to embark on a journey of becoming a life-learner.

This journey of seeking wisdom will be more fascinating than any other.

"WE GET YOU": WORDS OF WISDOM

I have determined that you are responsible for your own learning. The program can only give as much as you are willing to DIG OUT. THE EFFORT MUST COME FROM YOU! No one will stand over you. SPOON FEEDING IS NOT AN OPTION!!

In this profession as in any, learning is lifelong. If you do not believe that you will not feel successful. You must make a conscious effort to avoid burn out. You avoid burn out by keeping a balance. You will burn out or become an alcoholic if you do not.

KRIS RASMUSSEN, R.N. BSc, **Queen's University**
M.N., **Dalhousie University**
DIPLOMA PRIMARY CARE, N.P. **University of Calgary**

My biggest regret from college was not taking enough mathematics courses before going to university (especially Statistics), because I would have had much greater success. However, that being said, I would encourage students to travel abroad if they can during their breaks or for a semester (let us academics remember that it is an affordable goal in an 'ideal' world). Traveling will not ideally benefit a student in the sciences with achieving small goals in their major. For example, small goals could be completing course requirements in your field of study. Large goals of learning can be achieved by traveling. Large goals, like taking a semester to study in Nairobi, will make you a 'life-learner'. It will broaden your life experience, which will enrich your career and future apart from university. Achieving the big goal in university outweighs the small goal. It should always be the goal of a student to become a 'life-learner'.

BENJAMIN POLAK, Professor of Economics and Management, **Yale University**

Ph.D Economics, **Harvard University**. *Thesis: Problems from the History of Capital Markets*

M.A History, **Northwestern University**. *Thesis: Rinderpest and Kenya in the 1890s*

B.A. Economics (first class honors), **Cambridge University (Trinity College)**

Dissertation: Agricultural Credit and Rural Differentiation in Highland Kenya

Adaptability is the key to survival in any program at university. I meet so many students that complain their first year of university is different from high school. Don't be fooled. It is not even the same world. It is important not to look backward and complain about what has changed, but to look forward and adapt yourself to those changes and guarantee your success.

BEN BENSON, BSc Physics
BSc Computer Science, Minors in both Astronomy and Philosophy

My advice is to review your notes everyday so that you are properly prepared for finals. If you are cramming right before finals you will not know the material when you write the very important exam. I wish I had not just attended university with the attitude of just passing.

ANN POWER, B.A. Economics, **St. LaSalle University (Philippines)**

It took me a while to get there. I went to university for eight years. I took English, then majored in psychology, then halfway through I finally relented and talked to a dean about my future. He suggested that I major in Linguistics. That field was foreign to me, but it was challenging and I loved it.

SHARON BEERE, B.A. in Linguistics, **Brock University**

Your goals and dreams may change over time, but that is all right. Your goals and dreams may be refined overtime. You may not end up where you first wanted to—you may end up in a much better place.

GLEN-MARY CHRISTOPHER, B.A. English, BSc Nursing
University of Manitoba

Biggest regret in university: not finding out more about profs before registering for courses. Really ponder what level of teaching you want to do. I went through the Elementary stream, but was more geared toward teaching older students. As a result, I felt bored and dissatisfied with the courses I took.

ALINA FLOCH, B.A., B.Ed. (Post Academic)

As a professor of Renewable Resources, I think students from high school need to come to university with three basic yet crucially important skills. If they have mastered these skills we can do anything with them, and help them get anywhere in life. Although they are not sexy, they are crucial:

1. Understanding Algebra.

2. Have an ability to write a five-paragraph essay: with proper structure, topics, and paragraphs.

3. Have an ability to be able to critically and strategically read.

Reading is a good skill; good reading is a fine skill. All information in those thick textbooks does not carry the same weight or importance. Catch the author's clues: BOLD HEADINGS, HIGHLIGHTING, EXPLANATIONS.

JEFFREY A. LOCKWOOD
Ph.D Epidemiology, **Louisiana State University**
B.S. Biology, **New Mexico Institute of Mining Technology**

Time Management is harder than you think. You need to be very flexible with your roommate.

JUDY JAY, B.S. K-12, Phys.Ed., **Indiana University**

Just about every thought in life is a collection of smaller thoughts. In order to live an authentic life, every first thought must not be an illusion. The collection of thoughts must be put together in a manner that makes the result valid. This is the logic part of philosophy. Seek formal logic classes if you are a philosophy major; formal logic classes should be taken as soon as possible in your studies.

DONALD HENDERSON, B.A. Philosophy, **Lakehead University**

Do what you think you're capable of, not what your advisor thinks you're capable of. I was advised to take only 13 credit hours my first semester, but I could have done more. I wish I'd taken more because I had to do 18 or 19 hours a semester to graduate in four years.

KELLY MAGNER, B.A. K-12 Art Ed.

Re: Deadlines:

In my career I listened to students provide lively recounts of reasons for tardy assignments. An overdue task becomes an albatross, heavier than 96K of lead. At each hearing, I observe how many hours went into the construction of panic—often thinking the hours spent in renegotiation of deadlines might be enough to finish the essay. I never received a late composition of such brilliance that the wait was worth the words. When classes begin, build a fire-walled timetable to target product due dates at least one week to actual due date. Scare an instructor and turn in an assignment early. In the event of emergency, lingering lattés won't bloat the stress load.

SHARILYN CALLIOU
Bachelor of Education, Secondary, Major Curriculum & Instruction, Faculty of Education, **University of Calgary**
Masters of Arts, Department of Educational Studies, **University of British Columbia**
Ph.D, Centre for the Study of Curriculum & Instruction, **University of British Columbia**

The really crucial issue that I wanted to share with you is the student's role in the learning environment. As a teacher, my most disheartening experiences have been when a class was not fully engaged with the course material. The culture from year to year in the same course can be highly variable, depending on the mix of student personalities. In short, students can influence the learning environment tremendously by bringing their energy and enthusiasm to every class, and in turn, help instructors unleash their enthusiasm and desire to share their knowledge.

I hope you will discuss this concept with your fellow students, and in this way, do your part to build a strong learning environment that will support college initiatives on this front. In other words, the learning environment is a partnership between students, faculty, and the institution.

Dean of Arts & Science, **University of Saskatchewan**

Don't skip classes. It makes things easier; you'll know what your profs like, their style.

RYAN LYMAN, BSc Computer Science, **Bluffton College**

TIPS FROM UNCLE MICHAEL, THE SCHOOL PRINCIPAL:

1) *Attend all lectures, instead of trying to catch up on stuff from others.*
2) *Do early research.*
3) *Read only relative chapters to the topic on hand on books that are suggested for research.*
4) *Try to read up on topics before they are scheduled.*
5) *Most lecturers place emphasis on certain topics. Be sensitive to hints for exam questions and through research of past papers try to see trends of questions.*
6) *Become involved in some student activities – share your talents and gifts with others – they are not yours to keep.*
7) *Be disciplined about sleep time.*
8) *Always find time for God through daily prayers and weekend Mass or service.*
9) *When in need of help, whether it is study or personal problems seek early help.*
10) *It's a good idea to chat with those a year ahead of your program to see if you can get any tips.*
11) *Avoid company that is headed in a direction that makes you uncomfortable. There are many fish in the sea.*
12) *Visit home as frequently as possible and discuss your experiences with parents.*

Hope you continue to enjoy your teaching and friends. Just love them all and judge them not.

MICHAEL SAMUEL, B.A. (Gen. Hons.), **National University of Ireland,** Dip. Ed., **University of West Indies**

Everything matters; the little things matter. Putting effort into your assignments will pay off in the real working world. You learn something from each task that you accomplish. Your work ethic is a reflection of who you are.

L. ROGALSKY, Freelance Graphic Artist

I wish I had crammed less. It's easier said than done—but regular, consistent study (even in small amounts) is far more effective than long, compressed late-night cram sessions. Sure, cramming may help you pass the test, but it's highly unlikely that the information will stick with you much beyond that afternoon. I wish I had gone to my professors for help more often. The fact that several of my classes were huge (200-350 students) made me somewhat reluctant to approach the professors for help. However, as I found out later, most of them really are approachable, available, and one of the best resources for helping you to understand the important material.

JAMES, BSc, Medical Student

I wish my students had a better mathematical background (Calculus, Algebra). It seems that many of them are coming into college with weak mathematical skills. This will affect greatly their ability to comprehend and understand the teachings in Statistical courses. A successful understanding of statistics is crucial for success in the area of forestry, especially if they want to advance to graduate studies. Just because a student is in a science geared program does not mean they do not need writing skills. They need to know how to write effectively also. Both of these skills are important to have in order to succeed in the field of forestry.

DR. HAN CHEN
Ph.D Applied Forest Ecology, **University of British Columbia**
M.Sc. Forest Ecology, **Nanjing Forestry University, China**
Diploma, Forest Management, **Hefei Forestry School, China**

Ignore everything that you are taught because your job will be on-the-job training!

ROXANNE CROSWELL, Food & Nutrition Management Diploma, **Kelsey Campus, SIAST**

You don't know as much as you think you know. In high school, you think you know everything. There's a guy who started working with us, who came from a two-year Associates degree. HE found out he didn't know very much.

DAVID, Tool & Die Apprenticeship

Students in the chiropractic field need to prepare themselves for the political dynamics of their field. They will be expected to prove metaphysics factually. If they are not ready for this paradym they may become frustrated, rather than continue to help those who need them.

DR. STUCKEL, BSc Anatomy, **University of Saskatchewan**
Doc. of Chiropractic, **North Western College of Chiropractic**

In the Philippines you are under the American education system, so whatever you take is useless or of no value to work in Canada, unless you are a priest or a nurse. If I wanted to work in the United States, I would only have to add Business Law and Taxation to my degree. In Canada, I was advised that I had to start from the beginning. So I disagreed and challenged this, but it cost a lot of money! That is why you see educated people working at McDonald's, as labourers or driving cabs in Canada.

ROGER, B. Comm. Accounting, **University of Manila, Philippines**

Don't worry about picking a major too early. If you aren't sure, then take a broad range of courses and see what peaks your interest. Be 'open minded' about your career options. Don't be afraid to change your major or alter your particular program of study to your own unique situation.

Additionally, consider double majoring or minoring in a humanities program. For instance, study history or philosophy along with that engineering or business program. Ideally college should prepare you for a career, but it should also give one a well-rounded classical education.

Phil Poinsatte, B.S. Chemical Engineering, **Notre Dame**
M.S. Chemical Engineering, **Toledo**
MBA, **Cleveland State**
Currently working for NASA

My biggest regret in my first year of university would be: trying too hard. I put so much into studying and it didn't pay off one bit!

CHRISTINA BEAUREGARD, Current Languages & Linguistics Student

The university should have a way to test their student to be sure they have the leadership to be a teacher; to be sure they have the talent to control twenty students at the time. Lots of students finish four years of university to fail at their first year of teaching because they cannot control their class. Then they have to go to work as a waitress. The written report that we have to do three times a year should be taught in the university curriculum. Then we are able to approach the parents we need the most in the interview. We should be taught how to take the curriculum and transform it in a program well-made for our students. The psychology they thought in the university is far from the reality of the new generation of children. They should change their concept with the 21st century. The more important subject should be how to make our students shut up and listen to the teacher. In the 20th century teachers were respected by parents and children, so it was easier to transfer your knowledge to your students. The university should change all the subjects and adapt them to the new needs of teachers.

MICHELLE, B.A .Education

Students now need more than just a factual knowledge base *to succeed in the mathematics program. They need to be creative, able to think by themselves and having coping skills to work through a problem. All students wanting to major in math need to have already taken advanced placement Calculus at the high school level. University is not about facts, it is about thinking.*

BENITO CHEN, Professor of Mathematics,
Wyoming University
Ph.D, **California Institute of Technology**

CHAPTER FIVE

College did not teach us about cyber world

"Wired and Global"

I remember how devastated I was in my first year of college when I stared in disbelief at my warped plastic computer disk that all of us naïve, doe-eyed students thought was invincible. My project for Public Administration—an annual budget proposal for a non-profit daycare—had taken me 25 hours to complete. This project would seal my scholastic fate in the most important class I would ever take in four years of college, and was saved on my floppy disc without any backup. As I looked down with complete dismay as the computer spit the disk toward me, a lab attendant broke the news gently that my software had "Asian flu". I just sat there in the computer lab weeping, until one of my classmates came to comfort me, thinking that I had just broke up with my boyfriend. I slowly assured her that it was much worse than an ex-boyfriend: my file had just been infected with the Asian flu. Being an upright southern Protestant, she immediately thought that maybe she should give me a lecture about avoiding promiscuity. Wiping away the tears, I lifted up the disc that looked melted. She was uncertain as to why the disc was causing me more grief than my ex-boyfriend. However, full of empathy, she whispered words of comfort.

Luckily my caring charismatic Political Studies professor saw my big brown eyes twitching in distress, and he asked for the disc—motioning without explanation to follow him down a threatening murky hall. I was so hopeful about the solution and trusting of my professor, that I did not question which dark room he was leading me to. We walked through a mysterious door, down a dusty flight of stairs and into the bowels of a basement, as he muttered how the halls reminded him of his "time" in Congress. Distressed about the possibility of failing his class, I did not want to engage in war stories about his days in Congress. However, the longer I followed him, the more intriguing his jaded stories became. Speaking softly with a voice that only the Godfather would use, he reminisced about budget debates in Congress; I was completely enamoured by his experiences in Washington.

After twenty minutes of walking in the mysterious bowels of the university basement, we entered a room where two pudgy looking boys sat glued to their monitors. Occasionally looking down to wipe off powdered-donut jelly from their hunting jackets that truly looked as though they had not been washed in a couple of weeks, the guys would giggle and point to someone trying to violate a downloading rule, while they monitored the computer lab.  Although I really wanted to mention to them that Stuff-Mart did have a $5 special on jackets that week (so that they wouldn't have to do laundry), I held back—because I knew instinctively that we were standing on "Information Systems hallowed ground". They were the geniuses behind the scenes, who kept computer lab accounts running and functional. They were the unknown campus heroes, who could block Internet violations as fast as your mother could use her spit to wipe your chin.

After my professor cleared his throat to gain their full attention, they turned towards me, looking suspiciously to assess the extent of emergency intruding on their domain. They viewed my salty stained cheeks covered by tears, and were able to gauge instinctively by my level of fear exactly what they were dealing with. They knew that they were my only hope for retrieving my information off of the dilapidated disc. They assured me that by the time they finished sucking the jelly out of their day-old powdered donuts, while sipping on their cheap tar-like coffee, my virus would be gone.

Although I was tempted to skeptically interrogate them as to whether or not they had truly fixed the disc, I reminded myself... that they had not showered recently, jelly from last Tuesday was still on their sweaters, and we were all in a dark basement room. They could also sniff—like a hungry lion picking up the scent of prey—that my only background in Computer Science was buying an outrageously priced desktop computer because it had a nifty silver stripe design down the edge!! Thank God that they not only saved my data, but chose to graciously ignore my vindictive letters to my ex.

Survival Tip #12:

Speak methodically and softly to computer majors... your online bank account, personal identity and scholastic records are all at risk, based on how you treat these melancholy-phlegmatic personalities who have the ability to dismantle the college's entire system database.

Computers are a very valuable commodity in college, which is why it is of the utmost importance to have a computer account. It is even wiser to have your own computer for college. Having one of the first Macintosh computers in my family home at the ripe old age of twelve, I was one of the few fortunate kids in my generation to become well acquainted with a computer years before the Internet boom. Now it is mandatory at most universities and colleges to purchase a computer account in the computer lab, if you do not already have a computer in your dorm room.

Little do you know, in your youthful innocence, that you may be sleeping with it in your bed—because there are only two desks in your dorm room, and you need one desk to hold the microwave that Mom thought would "save your life"—along with all of your bathroom supplies, towels, new underwear you buy every week from Stuff-Mart (so that you do not have to do laundry), your stereo, a television that you hide under a towel because it is against the rules to have one, and your last two take-out dinners that you were convinced would stay cold because they have not turned the heat up in the dorms since 1989.

The only detriment to having a computer tower or laptop in your dorm room, is THEFT.

Laptops are very expensive, and easily left behind or stolen on campus. Perhaps after realizing that you should not vacuum your computer as I did (as that is not an experience most would have), you should also purchase a notebook cable lock. Get a well-loved computer geek in your family to take a break from watching one of his "science in space" shows, to put a bios password on your computer. That way, if the hacker does not get your password on the first three tries, he or she will not gain access. Upgraded software, anti-virus programs, firewalls, spam-blockers and anti-spyware may be worth looking into.

The first thing that comes to mind when most of us hear the words "cyber world" is a frail, single young woman among thousands, looking for that one perfect man of supposedly two on the Internet. In fact, many women would testify of reading many profiles on websites that state, "I am an energetic, outdoor-oriented, single man looking for the last woman to ever have a first date with". As the 'technology generation', we are comfortable with cyber relationships and the casual lifestyle it provides us. However, a word to the wise—do a little digging before falling in love after phone call #2 along with text message #3!

Hint: *If a cyber-man actually tries to lure you with the old "I have a well-paying job"—he could be hiding the fact that he is actually 5'2" and the father of six kids, with an ex-wife nicknamed "Psycho" and a big rusty-colored shedding dog. He does not want to post a picture of the dog, because you will soon realize that the dog's grooming habits are more attractive than his (no offense to dog lovers: after feeding two fussy, overly-demanding tabby cats, who for three years have defiled and clawed my couch without shame, I am very tempted to go to the local pound and trade them in for a Shi'Tzu that will love me more than my last cyber-fling ever did!!)*

Although there are some "cyber woes" a person can encounter, I personally love looking up information online. It is convenient and quickly acquired, in comparison to driving around campus, finding a parking spot, and looking through magazine articles. That is why I have a "favorites" file filled with links that are great for researching. One of my favorite links is the online dictionary, because many of my best friends are smarty-pants writers and conversationalists. With Internet access, I am not left out of the loop trying to understand what on earth classically trained musicians are saying. My life is *much* more meaningful now that I've learned what a "refrain" is, and apparently the Russian composer Sergei Rachmaninoff is a household name? This whole time I thought his name was pronounced "rock-man-a-knock" and that he was one of the Russian professors at our college hired to teach International Studies.

Another reason I love the online dictionary is because I can quickly look up words when I am conversing online with other intellectuals, cyber male companions who have an impressive vocabulary, or the occasional online counselor who helps me discover why I only keep men at the 'cyber friend stage'. I personally thought it was because I feared paying more bills, along with tolerating smells I was not ready to endure, and the need to avoid hearing myself talk rhetorically. According to a well known Ph.D in Psychology, I have a commitment phobia... Huh?! Really?? Not an aversion to racking up a huge cellular

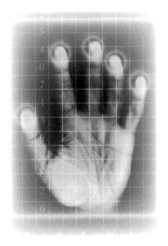

phone bill, having to babysit his dog while doing his laundry, with a reluctance to repeat myself in a nagging sort of way with a potential new man??

Hmmm, maybe she was right... I should pull out my trusty cyber dictionary:

American Heritage Dictionary - *Cite This Source*

pho·bi·a (fō′bē-ə) Pronunciation Key 🔊 ⊚

n.

1. A persistent, abnormal, and irrational fear of a specific thing or situation that compels one to avoid it, despite the awareness and reassurance that it is not dangerous.
2. A strong fear, dislike, or aversion.

APA: phobia. (n.d.). The American Heritage® Dictionary of the English Language, Fourth Edition. Retrieved October 14, 2006, from Dictionary.com website: http://dictionary.reference.com/browse/phobia

Dang, who knew that an online Ph.D could be so precisely accurate without ever having met me?! Just because people are online, does not mean that human nature has changed that drastically. We still have the same difficulties in relationships; there is just the added pain of being dehumanized now by cyber-love, cyber-friendships and cyber-life. It is not the fault of the technology as much as it is the people who have used it to replace human contact. I love the suggestions that I have read online, and feel the need to paraphrase some of them.

My good friends who did meet their mates online did so with two things in common. They were absolutely transparent with each other, offering church and family references if needed, and they made sure to visit each other soon after talking on the phone. It is the human contact that finalizes the potential of any relationship. Until then, couples and friends often have pseudo-intimacy online. According to relationship counselors, pseudo intimacy is an emotional attachment on a superficial level. However, some of us with a busy schedule and a desire for companionship often appreciate pseudo-intimacy more than real love, without realizing it. We have enjoyed the anonymity more than the personal growth that comes from being vulnerable.

I have also found in my own cyber-experience (by participating in a few chat rooms) that dating websites are the same as bars. Some men are just decent professional men or college students who do not like bars, trying to find 'the way' to meet someone kind and enjoyable, and some are seeking to cause trouble and prey on women. Some girls are on those websites to meet an American man so that they can get themselves a Green Card, and some girls love being able to talk to a man after work while sipping a coffee and wearing their jogging pants. It is mostly about convenience, fueled by the reality of globalization. Not all of the people are bad; not all of the people are good.

Survival Tip #13:

The key to deciphering the difference between the good and the bad is the level of transparency that you receive, and facing "red flags" when you see them.

I would earnestly warn Canadian girls to do a quick background check on the American men they are talking to, with inexpensive detective software. The only reason I suggest this is because in the era of terrorism, our Canadian passports are highly valuable!!! Make sure that he is indeed a legitimate American. It's very easy to locate a birth certificate online if you need to. Canadian women need to remember that a government agency in the United States does ongoing surveillance in chat rooms. You do not want to innocently become caught up in an attack against our current allies!

Cyber-world has not only aided and advanced academics; it has also created new socio-economical issues, pending legal issues and new political agendas. I would never want to give up all the advantages of retrieving income tax receipts and registering online. I have joked with older adult students who tell the dreaded *"...when I was young, we used a typewriter"* stories. It is always beneficial for students to learn, advance and grow; however, it is also important for college students to embrace humanity and all of its frailties. When students develop an understanding and compassion for others, their own personal identity becomes more clearly defined. It is compassion that reminds a student to 'humanize' people with whom they are speaking online.

For some reason, the anonymity of cyber-world combined with our fearlessness of retribution has created a shameless generation of young people engaging in cruel cyber-behaviour. We have changed from being simply impatient to downright rude and offensive. Therefore it is completely necessary that young people lead the way in restoring the rules of etiquette. Simply put: write online or text message words that you yourself would want to hear spoken to you. Remember that although there may not be physical ramifications for being obnoxious, there will be trail of casualties that you will regret one day. All of us, regardless of age, have regrets about something we said or sent by email or text messaging. This cyber-violation can be toned down to minimize occurrences with one simple step:

Think before writing.

Learning to talk nicely or appropriately online seems to be a rare attribute that only true professionals have developed. The reason for degrading communication is probably due to our sense of anonymity with the recent advancement of the Internet and socially accepted email practices. What is considered shaky ground is *when* to use certain vocabulary, and *how* to use email in different situations. My editor and friend is on the fringe of the 'baby boomers' generation, and although she nags me religiously to finish writing by our scheduled deadlines, I have learned the reason for her wanting me to properly complete projects: she is the most professionally responsible person I have encountered. She is very deliberate in how she handles her clients, speaking to them with the utmost respect.

Her conduct reminds me that my "Generation X" in North America has lost a valuable legacy that our baby-boomer parents tried to pass on to us. We have lost the art of etiquette, and have not understood what we have lost. Etiquette is simply the ability to address people properly online, in person, and by phone or mail. With all of these new electronic gadgets that create anonymity, people are acting and behaving with absolute disrespect that would make our great grandmothers jump with a sonic boom in their grave. Since I am not the one that shares this advice, but often receives it (because I am working hard on treating people properly!), I will simply call them "cyber-etiquette tips".

My editor, who acts professionally at all times, also has the coolest red candy machine in her office... with a funky little crane to pick up the candy from the glass container and place it in the gumball-looking slot where the candy falls out. Her first step in assisting my development in professionalism is to avoid holding our meetings in her office, where I am highly distracted by this novelty item. I am also assuming that one of the reasons she must OFTEN be repetitive with me, is because I am mesmerized by the funky lime green flipflop candles on display in a pile of California sand brought back from a family trip in the 60s.

"CYBER-ETIQUETTE TIPS":

1) WHEN EMAILING SOMEONE, REMEMBER: every student and professor you converse with is practice for how you will treat your future clients. How would you want to represent your business or yourself to your client? Would you want to lose the client because you wrote something in an email that you would have never told him or her in person at the office? Write online letters in a professional manner that offers your reader respect and dignity at all times. Some of these people have the capability of deciding how big your paycheck will be in the future. If you are like me and foolishly and hastily answered "Yes!" to the above question, I will then ask you what my editor always asks me: "Are you happy with treating people that way?" Would your grandmother not want to admit that she's related to you at your hometown coffee shop??

Clients + respect = paycheck
Professors + respect = EARNED respect

2) TRY THE 'SANDWICH APPROACH' FOR ALL SERIOUS EMAILS. That is where you start with positive statements, then address some key points in the middle that need rectification, and end the email with final positive comments. *(Well, that could have saved some of my friendships! I really wish I would have applied this principle much sooner!!)* In other words, DO NOT BURN BRIDGES UNNECESSARILY.

3) SOME CONVERSATIONS WITH PROFESSIONALS ARE BETTER DONE IN PERSON THAN BY EMAIL. If you are trying to discuss an important matter with clergy, professors, formal clients, new clients, and college administrators, call their office and book a proper meeting which you will arrive early for and always keep. This shows them that this meeting is valuable to you, with important issues needing to be addressed, and it reminds *you* that you are attending an important meeting. If you are a college student, DO NOT arrive at these scheduled meetings in casual attire. You are speaking with a professional; talk, dress, and act like a professional. **Your words and ideas will carry more weight when people see that you respect yourself.**

4) LIMIT YOUR HUMOUR IN EMAILS unless you are very close friends with that person. Over 90% percent of all communication is non-verbal. Email messages can easily be misconstrued and your brand of humour could be viewed as sarcasm or hostility, when you never intended it to. Professors do not need to receive these kinds of emails from you! Hold your wit for the classroom during a discussion that the professor actually wants to have (and avoid joking with the sheriff in your new town... or he will 'keep an eye' on you when you go rollerskating late Friday evening with your college friends). Make a habit of first saving the email to your computer, then reviewing it *one more time* before sending it. This way you will not send something you might later regret.

5) PHONE AND VERIFY THAT THEY RECEIVED YOUR EMAIL IF YOUR FUTURE IS DECIDED BY IT. I once sent an email with my 12-page essay attached, to my commerce professor. I assumed that the email was properly received, and that she would soon realize what a brilliant writer I was, awarding me an "A" average during that summer session class that I gave up a month of employment for. That one month of work would have covered the cost of my tuition! Then in the fall when I viewed my grades online, I noticed an 'INCOMPLETE FAILURE' attached to that class—at which moment I fell to my knees, begging God to smite me with lightening!! When I phoned the dean

about the 'incomplete', she informed me that it was my fault the professor did not receive my essay, and the 'incomplete' would stand. I then had to spend another six weeks at summer session to repeat the class, losing $3,000 in total (one of those life experiences that makes you weep at the altar in your hometown church).

Always *make sure* your professor has received your essay intact, and always print out two hard copies just in case. Always phone to make sure an employer received your resumé, and consider faxing or mailing as a backup. Have a backup plan that does not rely on your computer working perfectly that day. The "I couldn't print my essay" excuse is the same as "my dog ate my homework" excuse. In defense of the noble dog, I did come home one afternoon only to find my angst-ridden tabby cat chewing on my homework and my computer earphones. *Animals really do eat your homework!!!* Always allow for a 24-hour recovery time.

6) ALWAYS CHECK THE SPELLING IN YOUR EMAIL and remove words that are inappropriate for your reader to see on a professional level. Someone that is doing business with you may be religious, very political, or just downright unappreciative of your 'potty mouth'. Until I met my editor, it never once occurred to me that *"Hell", "Heck", "This sucks!"* and other similar phrases, are swear words in the professional business world. Yikes; one too many emails have gone forth like the desert wind, that I so wish I could take back now! It would have been wise to let my editor review one particular email before I sent it to my pastor's wife. I could have used in my freshman year: "A list of words to never use by email!" If you think the word may be "iffy"... DO NOT USE THEM!!!

Did you put the correct date on the cover letter of your resumé? When you send it online, always save it and then re-check the job details. I have learned that if you put the wrong contact name or job title on your resumé, it will get an instant DELETE. Be sure to proofread your piece.

7) MAKE SURE THE EMAIL IS GOING TO THE RIGHT PERSON. I remember not only receiving an email from a very young man about how he was going to sexually gratify a girl in every possible way; but that same day, I also received an email full of deep beautiful poetry by a man ready to commit, marry and love every inch of me for who I was and all that I am. *The only minor technicality* was that the first email came from a guy that was intended for his best friend (I didn't want to ask), and the second email was supposed to be sent to "Sharon". I replied to the first email to tell him that Jesus loves him, and that he does not have to spend his freshman year wallowing in debauchery; then I replied to the second man and told him that I was moved to tears, and very jealous of Sharon!!! Take a final look at all of the emails you send, and make sure you have entered the correct email address! I am sure that Sharon had a last name similar to mine. Always double check your emails to send to the right recipient.

8) ARE YOU AWARE THAT YOUR COWORKERS, CLASSMATES, BOSS, AND PARENTS CAN "SEE" YOUR BEHAVIOUR ONLINE? I was typing away frantically trying to make yet another stressful deadline for my editor (only because she promised to reward me with a vanilla latté—and I am cheaply bribed and bought) when a pop-up on the computer jumped in front of my screen. As I was cursing the day

pop-ups were invented, I noticed a picture of what I thought was one of my classmates at college. She was posted naked on one of those *"Passionate girls seeking sex"* websites. I knew from observing some of these girls in class that they were normally very shy girls, who rarely participated in group discussion—yet were willing to display their private body parts online. Hmmm, I thought... they are either very passive-aggressive, or have not realized that their classmates, bosses, fathers, and coworkers have now seen them naked. Email photos to people that you would never be embarrassed by. On the odd chance that they are sold dirt cheap, you will not have anything to dread.

9) If you say nagging, obnoxious things like me under pressure, and send emails that are way too blunt... TRY SENDING FREE E-CARDS. The FREE online e-cards are really your last resort for salvaging any relationship with your friends. When addressing a professional, a proper apology might be more appropriate. If the e-cards do not work with your friends, trust me—it was better than receiving a knock at your door from your best friend wanting to throw her cherry-flavored jello at you that she got from the emergency room. I suggest you try the e-card first! In the future, SAY LESS—LISTEN MORE!

10) EMAILS ARE NOT A SUBSTITUTE FOR PERSONAL TOUCH. In this new world of virtual romance, paying bills online, making appointments and filling out applications online, we have lost the art of "personal touch". I was very pleased to discover a book about what southern women know about flirting. The author is a *modern-day feminine genious!!!* Her brilliant book shows her readers how to reach people with a personal touch, such as handwritten cards, a friendly smile, and laughter that lingers delightfully in the air. Emails do not suffice in keeping relationships alive. You still need to make phone calls, send an occasional card, and have person-to-person contact over a quick coffee or lunch. Unless you have a personal touch in your relationships, it is only pseudo-intimacy that you have online.

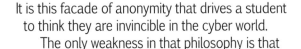

It is this facade of anonymity that drives a student to think they are invincible in the cyber world. The only weakness in that philosophy is that human nature has *not* radically changed at the same pace of technology. To combat every form of rule breaking, there are new rules created. This anonymity is at the root of the problem with "e-cheating". E-cheating is when a student is running out of time for an assignment, so they search the web for articles to cut and paste into their own essay. Then they leave those passages in without adding headers and footers, or properly documenting the source and the author, in the hopes that those brilliant words will sound like theirs!

Professors, on the other hand, become a little suspicious when they read 20 essays with exact word-for-word paragraphs. That professor can easily type in some of the key words in a search box the same way the students did, to see exactly where they found that information. "Old-school" professors call it PLAGIARISM. There is a horrible and PERMANENT lesson learned in college for plagiarism: the consequences for cyber-plagiarism in most colleges and universities is EXPULSION. The rule at most colleges and universities is:

"If you quote it, note it!"

The overall definitions of plagiarism are similar in all colleges; what is different is the application and prosecution if caught. Most colleges will expel you permanently from college if you are caught plagiarizing. If you go to the college website that you are attending, the website will have a 'homepage'. On this homepage are administrative links that you will need, and it will have rules by which the college follows. These rules differ from college to college, so you might want to quickly review them before you receive a $40 fine for 'not responding quickly enough' to a dean. If you type "plagiarism" in the search box, you will find the college's definition of plagiarism. They will also explain to you in detail the penalties for being caught plagiarizing.

Hmmm... let's check the online dictionary for clarification:

<u>WordNet</u> - <u>Cite This Source</u>
Plagiarism

n 1: a piece of writing that has been copied from someone else and is presented as being your own work 2: the act of plagiarizing; taking someone's words or ideas as if they were your own [syn: plagiarization, plagiarisation, piracy]

WordNet ® 2.0, © 2003 Princeton University

APA: Plagiarism. (n.d.). WordNet® 2.0. Retrieved October 15, 2006, from Dictionary.com website: http://dictionary.reference.com/browse/Plagiarism

There is a style guide and/or format in which colleges want you to quote a writer. Whether the paragraph comes from a book, magazine, or an article from a website, the source MUST be referred to in your essay after the quote, in a footnote or endnote that identifies precisely WHERE that quote came from, and also cited in the bibliography. Which format is used to quote the source is up to the guidelines set out by each college or the individual professor. Some professors want you to follow "APA" style formatting; some do not. Ask your professor about it the first day you are assigned a paper. A properly written bibliography will also be the determining factor between your B+ or an A+ mark. You don't have to quote commonly known facts such as, *"If you get caught plagiarizing, you will be escorted off the premises by the back of your pants"*. That is not common, but indeed a well-known fact.

The root of improperly organized essays—filled with too many quotes or unsourced works—reveals an inability to express thought in formal writing. Essay writing takes the same amount of effort and creativity as creative writing, but it is NOT creative writing. If you're having difficulty with writing an academic essay and don't know how to effectively write a bibliography, then you are in dire need of a 'writing' class BEFORE you get to college.

Even though a high school English class should be properly preparing you for a college level research essay, sometimes they do not. If you are struggling with essay writing, it is wisdom not to rely on what you were taught in high school. Take a formal writing class over the summer, or take a PRE-college English class that addresses these issues. Being unable to properly write a college paper will snowball until you suffocate in your third year. We were required in my freshman year of college to write seven-page research papers. That sounded like a mountain of work to me, considering I had thirteen other assignments due that week! Little did I realize that in my fourth year of college I would be required to write 20-page papers in my senior year.

You do not want to get kicked out of college in your final year because you were caught cyber-plagiarizing under pressure. By the time you hit your senior year, you could be a crabby insomniac that is so desperate to "cut and paste" in order to fill in page 12 and 13 of your 20-page paper, in the hopes that your professor won't catch the "filler"—all because you spent that extra half an hour doing laundry, while wishing the whole time that Stuff-Mart had not run out of your brand of underwear! PLAGIARIZING IS ONE OF THE BIGGEST RULES YOU CAN BREAK IN COLLEGE. Your mamma's 2-inch pie and her legendary flakey crust will not bail you out of this one!!!

The cyber community is now a permanent fixture in the global village. Even in the remote areas of Northern Canada on isolated outposts, young students usually have email accounts. There is no turning back the progression of technology. The Internet is the new form of project management, communication, research, and handling of daily activities. The only option for those seeking to survive, is to accept and progress with new technology. The only option the global village has now is to become wise with the USE of technology.

The new generation entering college is "young and wired". They have already embraced the field of technology without any hesitations that older adults may have. The only difference between the technology generation and those who are computer illiterate is whether they are willing to stay human. Regardless of how technologically advanced we become, we still have blood running through our veins. We still have a heart that can be broken. We are still capable of using words that could humiliate the human soul. We still need human contact and the simple reassurance of a caring smile. Technology is never as dangerous as the person using it. **Anonymity does not justify a selfish lifestyle**.

"WE GET YOU": WORDS OF WISDOM

I'm happy to help out a fellow Canadian. I am an oceanographer and I use technology a great deal in my research. As such I have to stay abreast of technological developments. For example, I use and build digital imaging systems designed to take pictures of very small organisms in the water column. I have to be aware of the latest developments in camera and computer technology to take advantage of recent advances. If I have one regret from my undergraduate days, it's that I never took any electrical engineering or computer programming courses!

I also use information technology to access information in my field ...online digital databases make it easy for me to access publications and reports. I think that as long as one's department/ school/college has the right support personnel to help smooth out any troubles that you might encounter, staying current with information isn't a stress at all.

MARK BENFIELD
Ph.D Wildlife and Fisheries, **Texas A&M University**
M.S. Biological Sciences, **University of Natal**
B.S., **University of Toronto**

Cyber world lacks the human contact that we really need. We need human touch. We need to know that someone values us. Being in university is so stressful that it is difficult to achieve that healthy balance of school and being with people.

BERNADINE NESS, B. Comm., finishing Human Resource Management,
University of Saskatchewan

I think the students are a little more prepared this day and age. I did not have a computer or laptop... you must have one and know how to use it to your advantage. I was not too bright on what a complete sentence was all about. You must have the ability and know-how on the writing part... what is a complete paragraph? I took on writing clinics and repeated English 100. Of course I was hunting down a tutor. I am one lucky person to find a good tutor. Kept this tutor for (2) years.

JOHN SWIFTWOLFE, B.A Indigenous Studies, B.A. Cree Linguistics,
FNUC Regina. Ekosi

you are not alone

A lot of students are too trusting and they leave their things on their desks in the library. Often these students will get up to look at some books on the shelf, and while they are simply looking for a book their laptop computer will be acquired by an opportunist who will relieve them of their property. Laptops are rarely recovered in a police investigation. My advice to freshman is to lock your dorm room at night, and even when you are walking down the hall to talk to one of your dorm buddies!!

JAN WOODS; Buffalo University Campus Police
M.S. Social Science, **University of Buffalo**

Students in the field of architecture need to realize before coming to university that they will be entering a field that is a SERVICE PROFESSION. Most of your life you will be working with people collaboratively, and will need to be able to articulate orally and in writing well. You are going to be using computers A LOT! You must be willing and interested in working with computers if you want to enter the architecture program. Many students enter the program with an old-fashioned view of the profession, not realizing there have been technological changes and advancements in the field.

JULIA W. SMYTH-PINNEY, M.Arch. (Architecture), **Harvard**

I use the internet all the time. However, I feel that time on the internet is always time taking away from my learning. I feel I learn more from books. Internet is good for networking. The Internet has become a place where people chat and share opinions. I need an alternative conduit for information. I see many students who write their major papers from Wikipedia (using the online encyclopedia as a major source) which is just laziness and lack of preparation. Students need to go to the library and learn how to dig out information. As a professor I want to see substantive bibliographies, proving that they have spent time learning from brilliant writers. Relying on power point and internet makes students mentally weak, numbing a student's ability to closely examine information.

ANDREW M. JOHNSTON, Associate Professor; **Carlton University**
B.A. **(Toronto)**
M.A. **(Yale)**
M. Philosophy **(Cambridge)**; Ph.D **(Cambridge)**

Introduce yourself to your professor. Do not just assume that they know you because they read your name off the class list. A little introduction and some friendly talk will go a long way. Take time to ask them questions. Email them. They'll remember you, and will appreciate your interest. They'll also respect you for it, especially because "freshies" never talk to their profs!

ANDREA, studied Music, **University of Saskatchewan**

The first invite a girl got was by a guy with whom she e-mailed, who came to her room and invited her to his room. He insisted on sex, and on her coming. She was shocked, and hadn't been exposed to that. She was polite, but told him that they won't ever be friends. They haven't talked since. For young girls, be prepared. Understand the world. It will entice you. If you're still a virgin by first year, it's very likely you'll lose it. Don't be naïve. Most of these guys are into MTV, pornography, etc. There were 3,000 registered sex offenders who left New Orleans.

LESLIE GENUIS, B.A. French, Theology, Minor in English,
Franciscan University of Steubenville;
B.Ed. French Immersion, **University of Regina**

Cyber technology may mean that some students really don't have to adjust much to the college subculture. Some students I talk to call their parents 4-5 times a day. Their circle of friends may be much smaller, but they keep the support system from their parents that may help cushion some college adjustments. Of course, the downside of this is that students may not be going through the anguish necessary to rely on their own resources. Late adolescence just isn't an easy time, and maybe we can't (and shouldn't) buffer all growing pains. It's just hard to move into an adult world and take on more and more responsibility. I'm not surprised that you've found sexual assault to be one of the most troubling experiences among the people you've interviewed. We get so many mixed messages about sexuality from musical lyrics to television programs like "Sex in the City." Rape on campuses seems to be reported more, and it's not safe for students to be out alone at night in many places.

MARY JO SCHNEIDER, Associate Professor (Anthropology)
Ph.D, **University of Missouri**

I don't have any quotes or tips other than I learned in university that when you want to change font, it isn't wise to highlight the entire document and accidentally hit enter. That was the same day that I learned the value of the 'SAVE' option.

MELANIE FREEMAN, B.A. major in Psychology, minor in Sociology, **University of Alberta**

In the digital world, always, and I mean ALWAYS, back up your work because one morning you will try to turn on your computer and... well, "try" is the operative word. Computers are a form of technology that is not 100% foolproof. Things go and when they do, it usually means your computer is gone too. Also, if you don't know much about how computers work, don't delete things that you are not sure about and think twice before deleting things you do know about. If you do delete unknown things, well, one morning you will try to turn on your computer and... well, you get the picture.

Thinking of pictures, print your digital images. It's easier to take a photo album to work than it is for a PC. You also wouldn't want to leave a PC in the lunch room for your co-workers to delete things on you. This also returns to point 1 about backing things up. If your computer goes and all of your digital pictures are on your now defunct computer... there goes baby's first steps.

GARY CHRISTOPHER, BSc Environmental Design
Finishing M.S. Environmental Design, **University of Manitoba**

Check out the university before you start. Check out safe and dangerous areas. Find students who live off-campus and talk to them, because some colleges treat you like you're on the outside if you're not in dorm. Ask your academic advisor for help in finding off-campus students. Check out drop rates of your instructors ahead of time. Three of us left one class a month after it started. Some dropped out the first week, and second week; I tried to stick it out, but couldn't. I had to write a letter to the academic advisor of Information Systems for information, but the professor wasn't removed.

MARCY, B.A. Information Systems, **University of Phoenix**

> Every campus is required to help inform victims of sexual assault on campus of what to do, because of the Federal CLERY law. It is good for parents and students to check out the campus website and become aware of crime prevention tips. Every victim has their first gut reaction in the situation about what to do, which sometimes overwhelms their knowledge of what they really know to do in these situations.
>
> S. MINNIS, M.S. Criminal Justice, **University of South Carolina**

> *Be careful! Who you think you know, you really DON'T know. Cyberspace is full of sexual deviants, weirdoes, whackos, and your run-of-the-mill creeps. And when you get into a discussion with someone, that someone doesn't necessarily have your good intentions in their mind.*
>
> *The internet is also a valuable learning tool. You can find out anything about anyone, but also remember, anyone can find out anything about you. Identity theft is the second most serious problem when it comes to the internet. Never share any personal information, even if you THINK you know who you're talking to. If you share credit card numbers, social insurance or security numbers, or even your date of birth and telephone number, identity thieves can assume your identity faster than it took you to enter your information into the computer. Then they can ruin your credit, your credibility, and most of all, they can ruin your lives.*
>
> SERGEANT DANA PRETZER, Weyburn Police Service

CHAPTER SIX

College did not teach us how to listen

Ears to Hear

My fondest, heartfelt childhood memory of my caring and adventurous mother, was experiencing an exciting summer road trip. To this day, Mom refuses to admit that she was a "wanna be" hippie who owned a green van with shag carpet, and a coffee-coloured cat who sat on the passenger side. We were on limited finances that summer, and always looking for new ways to have fun for free. Hopefully, my father (who shared custody of me with my mother) will not make me pay back the allowance he gave me when he reads this and finds out what I really did that summer!

I was enrolled in figure skating school for six weeks, since that is how Canadian girls who love winter spend their summers. After a gruelling 40-hour week of skating to break in a brand new pair of figure skates, then walking home to my boarding house in the scorching summer heat with nylons and a little skating skirt on—I phoned my mother and begged her to come visit me and take me away. I began to realize that my obsessive-compulsive need to earn medals over the summer was interfering with my laid-back personality, wanting to sit on a beach, wear funky flip-flops and talk about the "good old days". My mother reminded me that we had no money for travel, since my older brother was entering college in the fall—so we could only afford a holiday "gypsy-style".

These two words were a catalyst for my thrill-seeking active imagination. My young brilliant mind had an "Aha!" moment—I suggested that we drive down the highway towards the mountains, sneak into a cheap campsite late at night and sleep in the car, then watch the sunrise on the beach. It is easy to wake up early in the morning when you are almost six feet tall and trying to sleep in the back seat of a four-door car. I had dragged along a timid friend who would *never* be allowed to do such things—in the hopes that I could introduce her to my wonderful world of adventure. As we sat there on the cool grey northern beach, stoking the campfire, we roasted "koubassa" (sausage) on sticks from the forest, since we hadn't packed enough food for the next day! Although my friend was excited to learn that I was capable of building a fire from scratch, she also kept looking over her shoulder for park officials to interrogate us.

Sensing that my shy friend was hungry and apprehensive, my mother distracted her with loving animated stories. My mother was a very demonstrative storyteller, and each word she spoke was brought to life by her sparkling brown eyes. She was charming and humorous, with an ability to make even a tough old roughneck laugh out loud. Each story that she told was strategically placed like sandwich bread—before and after her "bumble bee story".

The Bumble Bee Story always started with how my gregarious grandmother (whose eyes often shined with her own writer's mischievousness) had ten rambunctious children. They were often curious thrillseekers, causing her to develop a profound amount of patience. One day she had all of her ten children in the lush meadows with her, picking juicy wild blueberries to eventually turn into delightful jam. My grandmother gasped with horror as she heard the sound of a swarm of angry bumblebees headed towards her precious children. She instinctively hustled her cubs like an angry mother bear, up and over a fence to safety. She naturally assumed that my mother, who was her oldest child with big sweet almond-shaped eyes, would surely not only listen and obey, but also help the trusting younger siblings to save themselves. She foolishly underestimated her oldest child's ability to be profusely stubborn. Yes, my mother was determined to be heady, unreasonable, unyielding, resolutely resistant to treatment...which is why it is in the best interest of a parent to rely on the youngest child!

As my grandmother soon realized the 'oldest child' was not following the others, she screamed with a resounding roar..."RUNNNN!!!!" My mother, being the detailed visionary—who to this day has to review an office's organizational chart to pick apart all of its future financial risks, comb each detail, assess whether the situation is fully realized, calculated, and if there is a possibility for restructuring—looked up with her intriguing eyes to ask,

"WHY??" Just as she said those haunting words, she was engulfed by a swarm of furious bees that were raging like a torrent towards her. She came home with 39 bee stings and painful welts all over her body, with enough story material to keep repeating this incident at every possible campfire that could and will exist.

It is a good thing that she is a tough survivor, because many adults would not have endured such an experience. This story does backfire on her when she nags me to wear winter boots—*because I am an adult that knows better than to wear flip-flops in the snow*. As the woman who allowed herself to be attacked by bumble bees is constantly repeating her winter advice, I often twitch in disbelief!

However, after entering college I began to highly value her practical advice, recovering from bronchitis six times. My roommates, who were quickly introduced to my mother's bumble bee story, would continually remind me that genetics were indeed repetitive... as we were driving free in the wind without a care in the world on one of our trips that *we* could not afford! The bumble bee story has caused such resounding fear in a vast amount of my friends, that we've all decided to avoid any forms of hiking in the bush, including berry picking. As I griped about my mother's favourite story on our road trip, they would often whisper to each other, "If only she had listened!"

As I have aged, I've discovered that *LISTENING* is not as easy as *HEARING*. I have learned that the *skill* of listening is much more valuable and important to develop as you pursue your future endeavors. My own personal regret about university was not listening intensely. I regret sitting in math classes staring at the boards with glazed eyes and refusing to listen, because I thought statistically it was hopeless for me to achieve such a monstrous goal as earning an "A" average in Calculus. It is absolutely astounding how many times I have gone to class, heard the Prof, and went home without remembering the point of the lecture. College did not teach me to listen—college taught me to hear.

The word 'HEAR' in the dictionary means "to be able to perceive sound". The word 'LISTEN' in the common dictionary means "to make an effort to hear something".

So, if you want to sit and simply "perceive sound" in a class that you are paying for, that is fine. If you want to perceive sound in your relationships over the dinner table while enjoying a delightful entrée, that is your choice. If you only want to perceive sound when someone is asking for help and challenging your soul, that too is legal. "Listening" means to make an effort to grasp and understand what is being said to you, through any form of communication. If you want to be a mature listener, you will not only have to make an effort, but you will need a strategy.

Listening in college has four basic components which students must master to fully grasp what is being said to them and produce positive results from the "listening encounter". To become a successful listener, a student must grasp the art of observation, investigate each angle, engage in meaningful reflection, and experience tangibly what they are learning.

A valuable habit to develop while learning to listen, is to OBSERVE. If only 10% of communication is verbal, then you will need to rely on observation of mannerisms, voice influction, facial expression, and physical habits, to perceive and hear what the person is really saying and communicating. This principle applies in the classroom, while talking to professors in their office, and in dealing with classmates and co-workers.

Survival Tip #14:

"Observing your math professor" does not mean repeatedly asking yourself for 30 minutes why no one has ever explained to him that lime green golf pants, and a burgundy golf shirt, high top runners and a coffee mug from the gas station, does not seem match his fuzzy grey caterpillar looking eyebrows that seem to bounce up and down as he talks.

Fruitful observation is when you watch attentively. "Observation" is to become aware of what you are learning, especially through careful and directed attention. Pay attention to what is being written on the chalkboard, or on the slide presentation. Pay attention to the professor when he or she says, "This could be a possible exam question." Most professors want you to do well in school; however, they want you to do well because you have learned to research, work hard, and listen.

I remember my father telling me often to write a proper essay, not poetry. I also remember him telling me to pay my bills and not spend all my money on pizza.

I clearly remember being told to pay attention to what a professor's style is, by reading some of his publications—rather than showing my professor how brilliant I was with my own unique written-the-night-before-it-was-due style. For some reason Dad was right, and now I am trying lose some weight from all that pizza, working full time to pay off the pizza debt, and re-learning how to write properly before publishing any articles academically.

If professors are giving you constructive criticism about your essays and papers, they are genuinely trying to help you. The intent is not to 'rob you of your future' because 'the professor lacks enlightenment'; so be humble enough to receive their advice, observe your errors, and learn how to correct yourself as you continue to write. Your professor is not a little green narbly character from a movie stirring swamp stew for you, trying to teach you how to levitate if you stay focused. The professor is simply encouraging you to advance as a well respected intellect in your field of study. If your professor has a Ph.D, those letters were earned. Anyone who has gone to college and university knows just how hard it is to complete a Ph.D Your professor has much to offer you, even if you do think that they are "sleepers". *(CODE: for so boring that they make your accounting boyfriend with mismatched socks picking lint off of his jogging pants look exciting!)*

As students develop abilities of observation, their need for thorough investigation of people and information will follow. **Investigation is an art.** The art of truly hearing information properly and retaining it comes from valuing proper investigation. Young freshmen often seem to swim in deep waters of investigation, floundering and spitting out water from the salty sea. Seniors watch with sympathy while sitting on the library couch, sipping coffee that they snuck by the 'library lady' who usually has eyes like a hawk.

Often, freshmen do not know how to do proper research in a university library. They often borrow old irrelevant books, or simply try to keep updated with the World Wide Web. Although using information from the Internet is a common practice these days, it is NOT a substitute for books. Web searching can be just as time consuming if you are unfamiliar with locating relevant information online, such as government documents, published articles, and press releases. Students who come straight from high school to enter college also have a singular mindset when writing their essays; in short, their research is biased towards proving their point that they refuse to question. **At the college level, a student is required to think through an argument.**

Survival Tip #15:

Successful investigation is not achieved because you learned how to download all your favorite study tunes, and convinced your roommate to join you in a game of pool until midnight because academic researching is for chumps.

Since your roommate has just lost four games in a row, he is now obligated to fulfill his part of the bet by doing your research for you. Investigate the material yourself, you hustling pool shark! In most colleges and universities, the library offers courses on how to properly use the library and how to properly research. These classes, although somewhat boring, will help you lay a research foundation in your scholastic life for the next four to eight years. Ask the librarian questions, spending the adequate amount of time going over sources. While you are reading, write down the quote and the bibliography while in the library on one of those coloured recipe cards that you bought dirt-cheap from Stuff-Mart (along with a new hair dryer, fuzzy bunny slippers, a new MP3 player, 19 packs of fresh underwear to avoid laundry, gummy bears to sneak into the library, and a door-size poster of a sexy cowboy (good choice, my female friends!) or that blonde bombshell.

Investigation is a learned skill that students acquire by inspecting details, and examining information systematically. It is a skill that requires patience and a capability to truthfully state the facts. It is very important if you are in the field of science to ask the professor how labs and studies are to be conducted. Ask professors if they prefer to have their works cited. Some professors do not mind you quoting one of their reviews properly; others mind having their reviews as one of your sources in your essay. Ask the professor what they are looking for *before* you submit the assignment—not after.

Learning from failure is only an option that comes after learning from success.

Whether you have looked down the road of life and envisioned your future or not, one reality holds true in many fields: nothing is more frustrating than working alongside a coworker who will not listen and thinks *they* are

the super-employee at their job! Nothing is worse than *being* that employee who "knows everything", because you will lose the ability to problem-solve creatively with that destructive attitude. Effective teamwork with management is achieved by listening to what is expected of you to reach the required result. You will be hired to accomplish tasks that are not necessarily in your job description. Your employer will not want to repeat themselves continually because you could not grasp what they expected.

When you have a job while attending college or after you have graduated, employers will train you for that new position. It is then your responsibility to improve your skills, investigate new techniques and achieve new goals, to produce results. All of this training for your career can start in your first year of college.

Primary investigation at college is knowing what you need to know to achieve success on a scholastic assignment. As a student matures, they develop an eye for detail and soon appreciate the skills that others have. Properly investigating what people have to offer enables a student to utilize resources wisely. Furthermore, a student who has learned to "listen by investigation" will do well as a team player in any group project. Listening requires your ability to think and consciously hear what is being said around you, and it is the most important skill you will develop in college.

Part of hearing all that is being discussed when you listen is done by purposeful REFLECTION. Wise people are known for thinking through concepts. My grandfather often said, "There are few thinkers amongst us." And that is so true in college! Most college and university students just learn to regurgitate what the professor tells them, or philosophically subscribe to whatever the latest theory is. "The purpose of undergraduate work," often stated by professors, "is just a time of repeating and researching what was said." Apparently the real thinking comes from graduate school, where a student works on their masters. That is odd, considering some billionaires in the United States who are in the computer industry did not make it to graduate school.

Learning to reflect and retain ideas will develop innovative problem-solving abilities that so few seem to have in the work force. *Be above the rest and learn to think.* Your capacity to analyze problems presented to you will help you find solutions that are beneficial for others. Often, meaningful reflection can prevent future problems. Abstract theory is not helpful in a time of crisis if it is not practical enough to meet a need.

> ### Survival Tip #16:
>
> *Reflection is <u>not</u> the ability to think through a perfect strategy to torture your "type-A" personality roommate, inventing the most perfect diabolical payback in history!!*

One evening my roommate and I were doing dishes together, and she kept putting the forks back into the water. I was shocked and dismayed, because I thought I had already "stepped up to the plate" by helping her do dishes. I was the one that wanted to buy a pack of 300 paper plates so that we would never have to do dishes! Sensing my impending mutiny and the contorted grimace consuming my entire face, shoulders and arms, her voice softened to comfort my sense of rejection. Watching my roommate scratch off flecks of macaroni, I asked her what demon she had succumbed to, making her engage in such anal retentive behavior. She looked at me sternly as all oldest children in the family do, and snarked condescendingly, "Can you go to sleep at night, and rest peacefully knowing that you missed all these chunky spots??!" I knew at that moment—the only way to diffuse this argument was to blatantly lie and answer no...I *would* be up all night knowing that there are spots on my forks. (I seriously wonder at times if the "oldest child" wakes up in the morning hearing a raspy deep voice calling, "*I AM YOUR FATHER...COME TO THE DARK SIDE!*")

The next evening as she left for work, I sat down on the living room floor in my plaid pajama bottoms, black undershirt, bare feet, a good cup of coffee, and my roommate's favorite bag of chocolate chip cookies. I pulled out *every* cookie, lining each one in a row. While watching television, I meticulously picked out every chocolate chip from each cookie. After eating all of the chocolate chips, I placed the chip-less cookies back in the cookie bag, rolled the edges up exactly the way she insisted, and put the cookie bag back in her cupboard that I knew was off-limits.

When she returned home after work, she came into the living room with the most horrified look that I had ever witnessed. It was more contorted than the day I told her that I might have forgotten to pay the phone bill... her expression was even more contorted than the day we both got our history exams back and she saw my perfect score plus 5% for getting the bonus question, when she knew clearly that I had not studied. In typical 'oldest child' fashion, she whispered, "Uhh, are we fighting?" as she shook the cookie bag, trying to catch my attention.

"Hmmm," I responded chillingly, "I don't think so, I am feeling well rested!" I assured her.

"*Henderson*—w-w-why would you do this???" she stuttered, with a heightened level of agitation.

"Ohhh," I responded, "I was reflecting about what you said... how I would sleep better at night, knowing there weren't any spots on the forks. Then I decided that I should remove all the spots from the cookies, to prevent contamination, and you were right—I really do sleep better!"

Although that level of sheer diabolical brilliance only follows hours of deep personal reflection, *academic* reflection has a slightly different application, involving non-hostile elements. Reflection is a mental concentration; a careful consideration. Some students are natural thinkers who often have an easier time thinking about a task—than actually *working* on it and *finishing* the task. There are a group of students, however, that rarely reflect on publications or facts they have researched. Think through your essay; view information from every angle. Think through the introduction, body, and conclusion. Review your course syllabus and highlight potential final exam essay questions.

Prepare your essay question in your mind before writing it in the final exam. If you are mentally prepared for the final exam, it is easier to learn detailed facts, and memorize dates, policies and formulas, to 'flush out' your essay answer. Be prepared with powerful one-sentence statements that will impact the marker of an exam question. Reflect before completing a creative writing assignment, and ask yourself what you want to say and learn. Each creative assignment often enlightens the reader and the writer equally. That is how a writer and reader become intertwined.

Reflection is a thought or an opinion resulting from such consideration. It is the result of reflection that allows you intellectually to agree or disagree with the works cited. Not every student has to believe exactly what the professor believes in order to receive an "A" on a college paper—as long as that college paper is well-written. Reflection allows a student the time needed to understand an arugment in an article and decide whether to discredit or prove the argument. On occasion, there have been intellects who are too insecure to be challenged. However, this is an exception rather than the rule.

I have known a few students who had a difference of opinion with their professors, and received lower grades. I personally challenged a professor who would not allow me to write my own political view of the Chechnya situation, because he idolized the United Nations. This tunnel vision of his beliefs blinded him, and I was proved right a few short years later. Although I had regrets of backing down from our dispute, I was empowered by my ability to maintain my insight. It is better to be secure in your own thoughts than to be cowardly because a professor won't let you write your essay with a different view. Although you make take a lower grade, you will sleep better at night! It takes great wisdom to know WHEN to speak, and WHEN to avoid confrontations that only serve a destructive purpose.

True listeners learn by experience. Learning is a lifelong journey; therefore a lot of what you discover has to be *lived*, not just read about. What are you speaking over yourself? What is your mind learning to listen to, over and over again? Thoughts are powerful and have a louder voice than your peers or employers. What kind of internal dialog is occurring in your head when you attend college? Do you tell yourself you are a failure, and you're never going to finish your degree? Do you base all of your future plans on a few past failures and bad experiences? Are you basing all of your career ideas solely on your limited frame of reference?

Do you tell yourself that you are competitive, and well able to handle the next assignment? Most college students are blossoming into young adults, and their ego is very fragile and soft while they are enduring the first year of pressure. The most difficult thing to listen to while attending university is students who continually speak fear, constantly reminding you how they are going to fail their next exam. You will not win many friends and companions if you are always negative and self destructive, because that kind of conversation and behavior is energy-depleting. If you talk and act like a failure, you may be encouraging your friends to talk and act that way. That is why it's always a good idea even in the beginning of college to seek friends that act as a catalyst for your success.

It is never too early to seek out a mentor or counsellor who can meet with you consistently, who has been where you have been and can offer you experienced and qualified input. You should be open and honest with leaders who are in relationship with you, for the purpose of your advancement. You should allow them to direct you spiritually, emotionally and scholastically, without exhausting them because you have not made an effort to follow any of their advice. Mature adults are capable of listening to constructive criticism and practical suggestions. As a mature adult, you will be expected to be transparent with many issues. Your mentors will help you discover your potential, and facilitate each issue you encounter with grace and dignity. Your reputation in university will not only be formed by your transcripts, but in how you deal with people as you complete forms, letters and administrative demands. If you cannot have a conversation about finances or scholastic matters with your mentors, then you are not mature. You should also treat them well, listening intently for ways to bless and thank them. Write a thoughtful note of appreciation to your mentor, or send a card expressing how they have helped you. Purchase a thoughtful gift, leaving them with good memory of you.

Many college students spend more time seeking to be understood, than seeking to understand! Many students miss out on experiencing life and learning by example, simply because they are too busy trying to convince everyone around them that they are a hopeless failure. The kind of person you should associate with is someone who understands and takes your goals seriously. These are people who respect your talents and encourage you. You don't have time to associate with people who enjoy being cynical about your future. Associating with successful people will help you avoid pitfalls while you are contending for your goals.

Learn from other people's mistakes and trials, by listening to their stories. If they had success in one area, try applying what you heard to your life. My grandmother used to say, **"Be a good example, or be a good bad example"**. In other words, she was warning us not to live life as a hypocrite, saying one thing and then doing another. That phrase taught me to look at all aspects of a person's life without getting caught up in distracting issues like prejuidice or preferences.

For example, one of the greatest kings remembered in history was King David. He told his soul *daily* to rejoice, not because he felt like it—but because God is good. His plans offer hope, and He wants you to prosper in every area of life! Have a passion for the God-given assignment of your life that overwhelms you daily. Even in university, there is time to hear from God on a daily basis. If you have time to stop for coffee on the way to your French History class, you have time to sit before an awesome God. Everyone in life has a success story, and everyone in life has a failure story.

Those of us who like to talk have learned the valuable lesson of talking less. Sometimes in college, it is much wiser to listen more.

THINGS TO AVOID SAYING IN CLASS: SPEAK LESS, LISTEN MORE!!

a) Screaming your French out loud in the language lab because you forgot that you have headphones on, all because the soft spoken French girl that you can barely hear on your tape is beginning to annoy you.

b) Do not put a treasure map on your R.A.'s (resident advisor) door, telling her that you will give her a clue each day as to where you placed your parental authorization forms.

c) Ear plugs are always the solution to ignore your roommate's fights over her cell phone with her soon-to-be-ex. You might not want to sing *"Love is a Battlefield"* in the background either.

e) If a professor catches you daydreaming in your Political Science class, never respond with "...uh, he had a long and fruitful presidency, sir..." especially if he was talking about the assassination of Abraham Lincoln. Wisdom might be to prepare a more general answer.

f) If you are bored easily, never ask your History professor to explain the Middle East crisis. Never!!!

g) Learn to nod when Engineering students are talking to you...it always makes them feel better, even though you understood none of their explanations!

h) You might not want to ask in your Honours Philosophy class if Alexander the Great was merely an only child with control issues...

i) Don't ask your American History professor if you can teach the class on the war of 1812.

Good students who are easily distracted by talkers and visual stimulation need to create an atmosphere that induces listening in class while attending university. If you are not alert in the morning and it takes you two hours to get moving, my advice to you is to avoid scheduling morning classes. Yes, in the real world you will wake up and go to work. However, university is not the real world. University is a time to learn and research and stretch your abilities, to think in the field you are seeking a career in. It is important to learn to wake up, but you can do that at your apartment, or at the gym. You do not have to roll out of bed and wake up in class. Take classes when you can best concentrate. Do not use your classes as a way to force yourself to be an adult. Do that on your own time at home. Practice getting up in the morning, hours before your class even begins.

Survival Tip #17:

Do not think that "learning by experience" means rolling out of bed, hitting your head on the wall, showing up at class with your jogging pants on backwards, spilling your fresh vanilla latté on your classmate, and realizing halfway through class that you forgot to brush your hair and teeth. Forget about changing majors—just change class times!

I remember as a first year Political Science major, the word 'day planner' seemed like a foreign policy word. Political Science classes were fun because the students often argued in class. Arguing and debating is very stimulating and intoxicating for any student who enjoys politics. However, this arguing does not particularly help a student get organized and learn the art of investigation. Ahhh, in first year when I was sweet and passionate about university, I purposed in my heart to attend every class, listen to every Prof, and read every inch of my 300-page textbook, plus the extra reading I found at the library. Where is that library? Gosh, I wonder if a majority of seniors even know that our university has one! If only that passion lasted past the first semester, keeping up with the extra reading I had acquired. After years of college, I have learned now that it is not the amount of information you acquire over the years at college that benefits you—it is what you have *retained and used* in practical applications that increases your knowledge base.

It is also imperative to listen and retain the information that is offered in class—through assignments, online research, and the media. This will prevent you from flipping through books frantically the night before your essay is due, drinking two litres of cola at 2:00 a.m. with your best friend, visually resembling a drug addict because you have consumed more caffeine than the legal limit allows. Avoid studying while you are lying on your bed, as your two tabby cats (who are the reason you are single) may decide that chasing your pen is more fun than shredding your new fuzzy pink mittens.

Another often overlooked suggestion in academia manuals is to open the expensive textbook (that costs more than your car) and read it. No, skimming the night before the final exam (because you discovered Thursday evening when you went past the final exam schedule posted up on the wall that your final exam was Friday morning) is really not the ideal way to retain information. I know after four cups of coffee that all your fantasies will feel attainable; however, the book will have to be read. This book will also have to be understood. If you are not processing the information that you feel you should, enlist the services of a tutor, talk to the prof's assistant, or make a weekly scheduled meeting with your professor.

Most professors don't mind helping students, IF they are prepared and have given advance notice of the topics needing clarification. At some point in their studies, all college students feel as though they are not properly processing all the information. It is imperative not to view that as a failure, but as an opportunity to make an effort to learn.

I have asked myself many times while sitting in my International Relations classes, why we as students always have to ask, "Why?!" It is the very reason we ask that enables us to achieve scholastically and be accepted into college; yet it seems to be the "Achilles heel" of most students, causing their demise. Is it possible to attend class and learn what the Professor is teaching, simply "because"?! There needs to be a reason WHY we are paying our tuition! However, if we attend class with the intent of listening rather than demanding, while making an effort to hear what another academic is expressing, perhaps that very choice could profoundly alter our abilities as budding professionals. The one revelation I received while attending my foreign policy classes was that *nations often seek to be heard, but so few seek to hear.* This frustration has only continued throughout the decades, as each generation has endured torture at the hands of ruthless governments "acting on behalf of their best interest", because they were fearful of speaking for themselves.

While we are making decisions in the workforce, we have to listen and see how our decisions are affecting everyone involved. By purposefully hearing people we are helping and working with, we will be able to overcome our own perceptions of how things should work. Having preconceived notions that are easily challenged while entering college will often disable your ability to view how your decisions affect those around you. There are decision-makers who create rules to make a social structure work smoothly. These people make rules according to their own personal judgement of social deviance.

We need to be very aware of how developing our listening skills will help our community grow and advance socially in the future. If we are not listening when we are young, we will take that willful ignorance into our careers. We will leave innocent people un-helped, and unheard. **By making an effort to listen to others, we will change our community with one lasting solution at a time.**

"WE GET YOU": WORDS OF WISDOM

Never ask a question you don't want to hear the answer to!
KATY PARSON, M.S. Ed. Middle School, endorsement Math & French

Listening effectively is actually quite difficult to do. We tend to filter everything through our own limited understanding or skewed expectations. But we are told to LISTEN all our lives, from parents to K-12 teachers and on. Curiously, though, the one type of listening I wish I had been taught to do was listen to myself. Too often, the talking side of things is unfortunate because the speaker never learned to listen to themselves and hear what nonsense they are saying. By the time many people learn to do this, however, it is often too late; they have let their mouth run away with drivel that causes confusion at best, and misery and mayhem at worst. As old as I am, I am still amazed and disheartened by what I sometimes hear myself say. But at least by listening, I have the chance to correct it.
LESLIE SARGENT JONES, Ph.D
Associate Dean, **South Carolina Honors College**
Associate Professor, Pharm., Phys., & Neuroscience
School of Medicine, University of South Carolina
Postdoctoral Fellow, Pharmacology, **Duke University**
Ph.D, **Northwestern University Medical School**
B.A. Psychology, **Bryn Mawr College**

Educators and researchers are right in the sense that they feel that mental issues faced by students are not their responsibility, because they are not qualified in the area of counseling and spiritual guidance. For example, if there is an accident you would prefer someone with first aid or medical training to help you. However, educators and researchers have a 'human responsibility' to be sensitive to the voiced psychological challenges faced by students and should guide them to proper areas of treatment if they are asked for help. It is a human responsibility, not a professional one.
DR. HEPBURN
BSc Chemistry, **University of Waterloo**
Ph.D, **University of Toronto**

Think through your decisions carefully. Spontaneity is good, but don't make impulsive decisions that have long-range implications. My girlfriend and I dated for a year and a half, and then got pregnant. We married immediately and dropped out 6 months later. We both worked, and she eventually went back to university. Four years later we separated, then divorced.

ALEX WASHINGTON, General Studies, **University of South Florida**

The door to learning is a continuous one that is never closed. Learning is a process; it is always open to those who diligently search. I don't believe that you can get all you need to survive within the four walls of any institution, because learning comes by experience. However, the institution empowers you with confidence to be able to deal with life circumstances. Since university is not for everyone, if you make it, at least you make it with a slight sense of confidence, so that you are at least slightly prepared. Truly, even biblically if you humble yourself, you will seek and find. A student must come with an openness of the mind and with a child-like spirit, humbling themselves; seeking, they will find.

ELO OLALEKAN, B.Ed., **University of Benin, Nigeria**
M.A. Religious Studies, **University of Jos, Nigeria**

I have had the benefit of learned instruction. I asked one female professor how she could possibly know so much about a topic. I thought there might be a shortcut. She replied that the only difference was time. "Time?" I asked. She explained that she had a dozen-plus years more than I in reading a topic. Her remark explained the position of her authority. Introductory reading lists are the foundation of lifelong learning. It's amazing what I've overheard students discuss; particularly comments about professorial ability or inability to teach. Hopefully, you'll never overhear instructors trashing your ability or inability to learn.

SHARILYN CALLIOU, Ph.D, **University of British Columbia**

Surround yourself with people who have good study habits. Pattern your study habits after them. Don't feel pressured to get into a frat or sorority.

JULIA KLUSMAN, B.S. Marketing, **FUS**

The best experience for students studying languages is to be immersed in the country, speaking the language a student is studying. Sometimes a student cannot afford this experience, and needs to find other cultural opportunities around them to learn. Listening to others from different countries helps you know another person rather than what you have to say. When you hear someone else talk, you get to hear them share their experiences and learn what they have been through. You will be able to hear what they have experienced. If you do not allow others to share their country's history, then it would be false to say that you understand their culture. Try to understand what other people are trying to tell you. Learning a person's language is not just being able to speak their language; it is about getting to know that person so that you both can communicate.

DR. SARA ORTEGA
Ph.D, **University of Puerto Rico**
D.R.I., M.A., B.A., **Université Stendhal**

I went to a community college. Be prepared for extreme language differences with your professors. I had Indian, German and Boston professors. In Physics, the Greek alphabet sounded completely different. Omega sounded deep and gruff, like "Omeger" with the Boston professor. In our small groups, the Indian professor said it completely different. It took weeks before we realized it was the same letter. One German teacher said, "Be careful about the pouver rule!" We wondered, "What pouver rule?" Then we realized it was "2 to the power of 10, etc."

FRITZ, M.E.T. - Mechanical Engineering Technology

We have at our college many opportunities for students wanting to learn a language. We have a language café where the students talk nothing but Spanish. By LISTENING over and over, they will learn to speak the language. There are just so many ways that they can learn a language if they are motivated.

DR. JOSE MINAY
Ph.D, M.A., **University of Tennessee, Knoxville**
B.A., **Lee College**

I went to high school on the native reserve, because that is what we all did. I did not have a goal in mind, and did not know back then that aboriginal people could have jobs. I went back to school after I had kids and a marriage that was not working. I went because my kids wanted me too. Now that I am a teacher I wish native aboriginal kids had goals. I also want them to listen when I am telling stories. Aboriginal people teach through their story-telling. If students are looking at my face and their eyes are not wandering, I know they are listening. I will not tolerate talking in my class. A couple of students have slept through my college lectures; even that is better than talking! If you are interrupting the flow of a conversation with your talking, or because you want to show the other person what you are thinking, you are not a good listener. I have only met 2 or 3 good listeners in my life. I am an elder, and have only met a couple of people who could listen well.

DOLORES WAWIA, Elder in Residence
M.Ed., **Lakehead University**
B.Ed., **Lakehead University**
B.A., **McMaster University**

I think we live in a culture that does not listen well. We have the media going 24 hours a day, the radio blaring, and all kinds of dialogue now talking or shouting their points. Active intentional listening skills are not being modeled to the younger generation. Some students that come to college are engaged and excited about their learning experience, while others are sleep walking through their four years of university. If you try to engage them into thinking creatively they almost resent you for not simply showing them what is necessary only to achieve a degree. They have passive engagement, not give and take dialogue where they share and communicate ideas. Critical thinking involves listening; it is an ongoing creative process.

HARRY G. HAMILTON
Ph.D Sociology, **University of Alabama**
M.A. Sociology, **University of Alabama**
B.A. Sociology, **University of Alabama**

you are not alone

I am so glad that I went to college when I was older. I did not get caught up in the childish need to be in an isolated gang. I went to listen and to learn. I knew what I wanted to do as a career.

JILLIAN WALKER, Massage Therapy Diploma, **Kelsey Campus, SIAST**

In the field of Physical Therapy, most, if not all, want to help people! A student entering this field must be well prepared to handle the rigor of the program which is comparable to medical school. It is a profession based on meeting the required needs of patients in a role of incredible caring and compassion. Part of their education requires developing good listening skills, and personal skills are a prerequisite for success.

MARILYN MOFFAT, Professor
B.S. in Physical Education/Education, **Queens College**
Certif. in Physical Therapy, **New York University**
M.A., Physical Therapy, **New York University**
Ph.D, Health Education, **New York University**

Give me 10 students that love ideas and we can change the world!! *Ideas are what change the world. Too many students come to college asking how they can get a job when they are done, and seek only a college diploma. Their listening skills are a product of what they learned before getting to college. Students are no longer taught well to listen and take notes. They have lost that skill and have become dependent on power point presentations, missing a large amount of details!! Relying solely on modern technology will hinder your skills as a learner who listens.*

DR. KEVIN L. CLAUSON, Professor, **Helms School of Government**
J.D. Law, **West Virginia University**
M.A. Political Science, **Marshall University**
B.A. International Affairs, B.A. Chemistry, **Marshall University**

CHAPTER SEVEN

College did not protect our ethics

G-Vegas: what goes on here, stays here!

I should have known, when I was scheduled to work as a cook at the hospital on "Barbecue Day" during one scorching summer, that by reason of default (everyone else took the day off) I would be asked to "man the barbecue". Very few cooks working in the kitchen liked Barbecue Day during the summer, because it required standing for hours in front of a huge smoky grill in 85 degree Fahrenheit weather, and asking excited yet weary customers if they would prefer a juicy German sausage or a charcoaled-to-perfection burger? It all sounded too daunting for an old Political Science major, because that is not how one envisions spending their summer after graduating. However, regardless of the complete disdain for standing in front of a hot dirty grill and wearing scrubs that look like pajamas, a very strange feeling came over me. Although I was apprehensive, a flush of exhilaration pulsed through my body. I am told that any human being, man or woman, gets a little peevish when they are given the tools to light a barbecue.

Due to my prissy-city-girl inadequacies, my overly detailed yet impeccably organized manager (who was raised out in the country) had to show me how to light the barbecue. As I drank my coffee and watched intently, she muttered the whole time that Prince Charming was not coming to sweep me off my feet or marry me purely to light the barbecue every summer. Although my marriage dreams were crushed in that one conversation with this jaded farm girl, I did learn how to light that stainless steel barbecue which quickly became a new delightful toy. I was going to question her angst about Prince Charming during my break, but decided to save my energy for a bag of yummy potato chips that offered me greater satisfaction. Besides, I was told by other farm girls that "Prince Charming" is only a notion city girls concocted, because they have way too much time on their hands.

As I petted the barbecue softly, becoming mesmerized by its heat and power, my eyes started to glass over... reminding my manager of all the endless possibilities that could arise from allowing me to cook. She decided after watching me talk fondly to my new silver toy that she should remind me how to use the fire extinguisher. I was convinced that sunny morning that I needed more heat and bigger flames. The colourful, flickering gas flames of a barbecue are an intoxicating and gratifying addiction to compulsive people such as myself. I insisted that my manager needed to send me the maintenance boys to crank up the heat—because the men I kept complaining to were ignoring me.

Their indifference resembled that of Confederate foot soldiers during the civil war, who wanted to ignore the great General Lee that cold frightful morning when the historical battle of Fredericksburg was fought. I knew when the maintenance dept. sent out the plumber to talk to me about the barbecue not really needing more heat, that they were 'yellow'. They wanted to avoid any more flames, like a bunch of frightened Yankees staring at "Stonewall" Jackson's troops. I kept whispering to myself repeatedly, as General Lee might while surveying the rolling hills of Virginia, that I had one mission and one mission only—the flames must reach three feet high!

When my manager came outside with her silver flask of water, the good Paula—the one on her way to heaven, the one who has taken Food Safe courses—knew that water poured on a propane fire would activate combustion. The good Paula knew instinctively that water would be a very bad idea! That's why I was secretly relieved that the hospital had tornado-proof glass windows between us and the customers in the cafeteria. The bad Paula—the one who wanted three foot flames at all costs—whispered to her boss, "That's right, pour that water on the barbecue!" Now in every crowd regardless of where it is, there will always be some 'scaredy-pants' nurse muttering nervously, *"Code Black?? I think it's a BOMB!!!"* Any time nurses see flames go three feet high near a young woman's face while she gleefully observes the phenomenon, they tend to panic.

There is a natural tendency for nurses to guard against bodily damage of a cherished employee (if it is not during their coffee break), which is the result of their training. My boss did later apologize for causing the bright red patch burned in the shape of a circle on my forehead. She jokingly assured me that it was a casualty of working on "Barbecue Day". I was so mesmerized by the flames of that barbecue, that I was eagerly willing to burn the eyebrows right off of my boss and coworkers, if that would get me three foot flames!

Hey, my boss doesn't need to wait for Prince Charming; she can already light her own barbecue. She also told me that eyebrows grow back! After seeing the resulting damage from my sense of empowerment that those beautiful flames gave me, I realized that college had not prepared me at all for the ethical choices that I would face at work. College trained us how to do the job—not necessarily what kind of employee we would be.

College also didn't prepare us to properly process thoughts about our employers, without saying them out loud! In fact, college didn't really prepare us for what we could or couldn't say—nor did it give us guidelines about how to improve our workplace without hurting someone. Change in some workplaces is necessary for the advancement of safety. Yet few young people know how to promote creative change in an ethical way. Young people tend to be zealous and want to see immediate results; the downside of this impatience is often long-term damage.

In short, we were taught career skills; not how to be professional. We did not value how our conduct affects our professionalism. Everyone that I have worked with has varying degrees of what is ethical to them, and has a different reason for being there. Ethical choices at work will be an extension of ethical choices made while attending college. That is why you should continually ask yourself, "where is my character right now?" For example: do I put MONEY, REPUTATION, AND FAME before God and charity towards my neighbors? That is why it is very important to make wise ethical decisions while attending college. What you do in college does not stay there!! What you do in college follows you to your career.

Looking back to my college days, I remember many rides as a passenger in my best friend's dilapidated red hatchback that was so small, I often banged my head on the roof. She often drove me around the neighbourhood, helping me search for a new adventure. She also felt the need to follow and protect me, because she was the "oldest child" and had to please my mother by preventing an unfortunate hospital emergency. As we drove around our college town, we unintentionally passed some bleak, dusty, needle-covered streets, with impoverished homeless people in search for food. It was then that I took a deep breath and prayed, asking God to help me graduate from university with a purpose and a soul. As we exited the freeway to return to campus, I sipped my latté silently. My stomach churned, and my mind wandered while listening to the soft worship music my friend often played that lingered in my ears. I gazed wistfully at the mustard yellow and jade green fields, as the crops waxed and waned with the wind. It was so serene, and the day had not yet been conquered by anyone.

I realized while we were driving that Generation X does not understand what true freedom means. The word *liberation* escapes our understanding like water that quickly evaporates in the summer sun. We don't understand what it means to stand "shoulder to shoulder" in unity with our sister or brother, fighting for the same cause. Generation X and Y, like many other deceived generations, has been indoctrinated with humanism. We have been taught that ethics are situational, and we have been exposed to a reality that is subjective. The result of this mindset is a generation that is very materialistic, willing to fight for their own way at any cost... any cost to our marriages, our children, our beliefs, and our identities. We are willing to fight legally for freedom of speech; however, the only speech that we want to be free is our own. We do not want teachers to question our morality and ideologies. In essence, we have become enslaved by our own self-will. Our ideologies have failed us—yet we abide by them anyways.

University will not teach you ethics; you need to BE ethical *before* you start university. Your ethics will define how you comprehend and follow the laws within your field of study and future career. Your major will be defined by your ethics. The pressures of college will not produce ethical thought and logic, nor will it enhance your character; it merely reveals the depths of your mind, whether pure or evil. Entering college is somewhat like entering a marriage; with new challenges, your personal habits will not grow worse or become better—they will merely be exposed. College will not transform you into who you want to be or not to be; the demands that are placed on you will merely reveal who you already are. In essence:

You will do college the way you do life.

Little did I know that our ritual of attending church, where we worshipped, would be the doorway to... expanding our ability to care? Little did I know in the frivolity of my youth, that prayer would inspire me to... help those in need who were all alone? It took me five years to learn the discipline of being quiet while attending school.

The art of teaching your mind to be quiet not only enables you to hear God speak, it enables you to hear yourself. It is impossible to look in a mirror without opening your eyes. It is impossible to hear yourself, if you are not quiet enough to listen. Thoughts and feelings are not useless; God has given them to us for a reason. God does not want to control your mind; He wants to share His thoughts with you. Books will change your opinion, and perhaps your views; but only Jesus Christ has the ability to change your heart. Only Jesus has the ability to change YOU.

In order for my best friend and me to pray for something bigger than ourselves, we had to allow our hearts to expand. We wanted to build our community, defend our nation, and pray for those we loved; but we didn't know where to start. In order to have the kind of impact that we desired in our community, we soon realized that we needed to spend four years in college doing more than just studying and earning a degree. We had four valuable years to define who we were, what we believed, and whether or not we were going to be humanitarians. We had the option of becoming givers of all that we had, or takers, stroking our own egos and caressing our dreams at the cost of others.

Taking from others until they are left with nothing only occurs when a young adult is living for themselves. This is why some students are challenged when they leave home for the first time and attend college or university. They must decide for themselves whether or not they are going to maintain the laws of God on their heart. I say this to students with fear and trembling; parents are not the one that students will answer to when they die. Make sure as a student that you have sought God about the call (your mission and destiny in life) and His will for your life. If you have not done this all through high school, make sure you do it before entering university and spending thousands upon thousands of dollars!!! I've calculated that I spent a minimum of $25,000 each year while attending university. Make sure that you are in the right program *before* you write your first cheque.

When you hear from God, provision will follow your vision. Your destiny is something you discover, not decide. It is a shame that not enough people are brave enough to pursue their destiny. Some students don't seek their destiny because they are fearful that they will be miserable. Some are fearful

you are not alone

that their destiny will require major changes, or requires contentment with where they are. Seeking our destiny should never be a fearful thing! Knowing our destiny is freeing, and allows us to relax and enjoy those around us. What is your God-given assignment? You know— those problems in your community that really bother you? You are called to fix those problems! You are not on this earth just to earn money, have a family, watch television, and then die. All of us are asked by God to improve our community, and when you are sensitive to the needs of others, you will understand.

I have learned this over the years while working with two older, unforgettable women in my department. Dagny is a gregarious blond woman with a smile that could wipe away tears. She would often tease me, to remind me that I am human like everyone around me. She also loves to play tricks on me! One day I was bragging about my impressive sales abilities that I thought were unmatchable. She went around the corner and phoned me with a disguised voice to order ten fish burgers, on a quiet Tuesday evening with very few customers. As I unsuspectingly prepared the order, I heard a giggle close by. Looking up, I saw mischievous blue eyes sparkling with delight as she envisioned my desolate evening trying to prove that I could indeed sell that much fish! (Mental note to self: keep well-known skills a secret.)

Annabelle is a steady compliment to her friend and a great balance for my coworkers and me, always reminding us to get some work done! She was the only woman I have ever known who has reverent respect for those in authority, yet is able to "shoot straight from the hip" when she speaks. She often took care of us with her sharing and stability. She offered her plums to me when I couldn't afford a staff meal, while reminding me that cowboys were nothing but a distraction! I will never forget my first encounter with her in the hospital elevator. I was leery of going to my job interview in her department, looking down sheepishly at my sneakers while waiting for my desired floor. She pointed to my coat, trying to make conversation and to get me to look up. She spoke kindly to me—yet she didn't even know me. I was so thankful for her compassion on that important day. She has taught me that when you look up rather than down at your shoes, you will see someone smiling at you.

Over the years, Annabelle and Dagny have taught me to build a community rather than pick it apart with my jaded disdain. They showed me that many employees can tear down a community, but very few can build one. They taught me by example to treat people at work with dignity and respect—that learning to care about who I work with and serve, simply makes work more enjoyable. There is nothing wrong with simply enjoying work and the people.

Laughing and enjoying life will not rob you of precious "career success" prepraration time. Being able to laugh daily with those around you *is* a career success. Being able to share your dreams with others and help them realize their own, is exciting. Your purpose in life called an assignment, and your life assignment is much greater than merely receiving an "A" in your Calculus class. Your assignment is not to change and rescue everyone. If God tells you to speak to someone, do it with discretion—you are there to learn. How will you succeed in school if you spend time helping others? Simple: you will maintain good grades by creating goals and using your time efficiently! You do not fail an exam because you volunteered for a Red Cross blood donors drive at your college. You will not fail college because you volunteered to do some hurricane relief preparations in your community, to help make your community safer in the event of a crisis. You fail an exam because you did not take time to review your notes after class every day.

Doing well in a class is a result of daily discipline. After class you need to read over your notes, and read the assignments given to you right away. If you want to be at the top of your classes and have mature life as a humanitarian, you will have to have a disciplined study life. Don't leave your assignments for the weekend, nor sacrifice all of your time volunteering. Simply learn the art of balance. If you will not tackle your college assignments on Tuesday evening, you will not tackle them on Friday evening. Learn to deal with your college and university assignments early in the week, so that you have time for volunteering and physical activity.

If you want to attend Wednesday night church service or Mass, work out a routine for getting your assignments and research done that afternoon. If you need the extra time, then skip dinner; fasting on Wednesday will not hurt you! You may even enjoy a delightful conversation with that little old woman that always sits in the back pew. She may very well enjoy the smell of chocolate that you smuggled in because you were hungry and have perfected the art of multi-tasking.

Hint: *As you sing hymns with chocolatey breath floating into the air, other students may become vexed while trying to worship because they're hungry!*

Survival Tip #18:

Do not go to the bathroom alone—you might get overpowered by some hungry college students trying to raid your purse for all the other goodies they know you have stashed there to hide from your roommate!

The idea of getting involved in something greater than yourself is not a radical suggestion; this is practical advice for students who are serious about making a difference with their lives. They discover where they need to go to help others. **Huge sacrifices for were made for you, and you can make some sacrifices in your lifestyle in order to live for others.** When you are bitter with your surroundings, it is because you forgot to thank all of those people who contributed to your successes. An attitude of gratitude creates an positive atmosphere.

Skip the movie on Friday evening if you are behind in your studies. Do all of your work first; then play. Don't play all weekend and then start late Sunday evening to do your course assignments! The habits you form in university are the habits that will follow you the rest of your life. If you are always late for class, I guarantee that you will be late for work. The advice and the quotes in this book come from experienced students who have learned some painful lessons. There is no need to learn them firsthand! Is it difficult to be spiritual and also be focused on university? Yes, you bet!! Will everyone in your church understand the sacrifice you are making? No... only a minority will understand. However, you probably have no idea of the sacrifices they are making in order to stay ethical themselves. The rewards for being diligent with spiritual development in your life will be worth it. You *can* do both, IF—and only if—you lead a disciplined lifestyle.

I remember sitting in chapel trying earnestly to listen to a man of God preach about 'vision', while being distracted by the conversation of a young freshman who was a beautiful southern belle, enamored with girlish delight about dating a very popular football player. She was giggling while talking to her admiring classmates, and writing notes to her boyfriend that was a senior. By the middle of chapel during that frosty cool spring morning, he was writing her earnestly about having sex that weekend. He was pressuring her to have sex that weekend, so that they could 'go to the next level with their relationship'. In the letter she explained that she did not know how, and that her and her parents were devote evangelicals that did not believe in premarital sex. That week, I prayed for this young naïve female freshman who went to university to find a Christian husband, but instead was ensnared by a senior taking advantage of her innocence.

Many young girls have lost their virginity against their will, been dismayed by unplanned pregnancies, and some have even died from sexually transmitted diseases while attending university. They were merely indifferent about the consequences resulting from new ethical situations that were present at college, which in no way resembled their hometown with the "down home" upbringing. Sadly, this true account with the young southern belle occurred during chapel time in a Christian university. There is nothing wrong with hoping to marry an educated man with the same faith that you have, and finding him at university. However, this girl decided that she would never find a potential life mate who shared the same values and goals that she did. She settled for an attractive man offering her crumbs. She settled for a young man that did not respect her upbringing, and he left her jaded. She would not be the wife that she desired to be, without unwanted insecurities. She did not firmly decide her convictions before attending university—and when a young man pressured her to comply with his desires, she felt too helpless to set personal boundaries.

Ethics are not just about a student's sexuality; they are basic guidelines for every decision a student will make. A young man may have a 4.0 GPA in engineering, but if he rapes a young girl while attending college, he could go to jail like other convicted criminals do. The judge won't excuse him because of a very high average in his major, with greater potential than any of the

other guys he went to high school with. College is *not* an oasis where crime doesn't matter, with a bunch of students on a deserted island competing at all cost to see who finishes with a million dollars in the end. The law must be followed on campus as it is in their hometown. If you break the law in your new town, you will be prosecuted and it will be publicized.

The only thing that will change is *which* laws, depending on which state university that you attend. Approximately 15% of college girls will be raped in a U.S. college and 8% in a Canadian college *(those that are reported).*

you are not alone

Sexual assault against young men occurs too, yet it often goes unreported. It seems to be overlooked and underprosecuted, which is a horrible tragedy for those young men who desperately need counseling because of their experience. They need to be brave enough to ask for help when needed.

For every assault reported, it is commonly said that there are five more that are not. Statistics show that rape on campus is often between peers—often referred to as 'date rape'. Sometimes friends feel that if they address the situation with local authorities, they will lose a friendship or suffer a social backlash that will come from the faculty or their classmates. Some do not want to report rape, because they are humiliated by not being handled in a sensitive way when they go to the police station to report it. The first reaction of a woman who has been assaulted is to shower, rather than go to the police. If anyone has been sexually assaulted, there are centers on campus to help a student with such a situation and help them write up the report (if they are ready to write a report), and offer counsel to the student.

All colleges in the United States will have a link on their website explaining how to prevent this kind of situation, and what to do if it occurs. Most campuses also have something called a SAFEWALK program. That is where a couple of students walk with a woman or man to their car at night. **I would highly advise freshmen students to walk with the SAFEWALK team or more than one peer to their car at night when they go to campus to study.** You may have to wait for them; but if you don't know the large campus well enough, you may get lost. Even if you tried to escape an attacker on campus, you may not know where to run for safety—enabling yourself to become a greater risk of being a victim. Consciously plan how you are going to protect yourself.

Another hot topic at colleges is THEFT. Some students do not share the same value system as you, and have a different 'understanding' about what they view as theft versus survival. All I know is, when all my candies, class notes, favorite music CD, and leather jacket are missing... hmm... somethin' just ain't right!!

Theft, I am told, has varying degrees in college. Some students don't mind returning to their dorm room to find everything missing that they just bought from Stuff-Mart—because that is the first time they have seen the floor and the back of their closet in weeks. Some students are so unorganized that they have no idea stuff is missing, until the chatty girl down the hall comes to borrow hairspray, or that ugly sweater from Mom that your roommate won't steal.

Other students have a tendency to want the ten dollars they had left in their jean pants. They need it to buy a coffee with their best friend, so they can talk about their roommate with loathing disdain because he is a donut-eating, conniving thief that would take your underwear if left in the dryer without supervision. If you have an older sister who has already stolen your boxers and favorite t-shirt because they are comfy, you have already been challenged by this dilemma and do not find the situation shocking. However, perhaps a trunk with a lock on it at the end of your dorm bed, or one bought from Stuff-Mart that fits under the bed might be a good idea.

Locks need to be bought for laptops too! A BIOS password should be installed, which makes life suck for thieves who stole your computer just to hack at your information. Apartment insurance might also be an option for those students coming to college with expensive toys. It even might be wisdom to lock up that pizza-smudged gaming console you brought to campus that is usually hidden in the sock drawer. Besides, some college students wear flipflops when there is snow on the ground; you might forget that you hid it in the sock drawer. Use a lock box since you only wear fussy socks to make your mother happy because every time she phones you, she thinks you're sniffling with another head cold. Also remember to lock your door when you leave your dorm room, even if it is just to go down the hall to tell your cool dorm mates about the new freshman girl who looks HOT in jogging pants!

Survival Tip #19:

Protecting your property while in dorms may not be as easy as buying a bunch of grapes to pelt your roommate with, every time they touch something of yours. You might want to actually use that key that they give you for the lock on your door that you didn't notice, because you were too busy looking out the window at the girl who has curves that make your knees weak.

Some students think that it is perfectly acceptable to skip labs and borrow notes. Other students are offended when asked, because they think that this is theft. Heck, when I was a Political Science major, students in my field were willing to sell their notes to the highest bidder and convince the professor to give us question hints for the exam. The government majors are often charismatic and charming, so the highest level of negotiations will always take place in those classes. Some of these students don't think it is unethical to tell their professor that their fourth grandmother just passed away again in Florida, and that's why it was absolutely imperative for them to travel to Daytona. They needed the weekend to grieve, instead of finishing the comparison essay of "the nation state" verses international law.

Here is a thought: *Why not tell the professor that you enjoyed his class and lecture?* Why not bring your professor a coffee WITHOUT using it for bribery purposes (unless it is a Law professor). Those professors will accept your coffee, have a stimulating and pleasant conversation with you, and then decisively fail you. They are a rare breed, and never to be taken lightly!

Some students do not think it is unethical to skip classes regularly and then ask a classmate what was taught for the past two weeks (that class starts way too early, and they are ill-prepared for the lecturing nuances of a post-graduate Berkley professor without caffeine in their nervous system before dawn). Some roommates think it is perfectly ethical to use your expensive shampoo and conditioner, and borrow your favorite sweater that you stole from your Dad's closet because you are still fighting with Mom. They do not think it is unethical to swipe *your* card at the cafeteria. Those are often the same roommates who think it is very unethical of *you* to glue a detailed list of all they have done wrong on the resident advisor's door. They don't understand that you are legitimately doing research on "velocity changes" incurred by inadequate anger management! Never try to reason with the shampoo-using roommate; they have perfected the glazed-over look when you question their humanity and suggest they search for their soul.

Survival Tip #20:

Instead, take all of their favorite snacks from their sock drawer, and find a new hiding spot (on the top shelf of their overstuffed closet), watching with delight as they search in vain for hours, refusing to ask for help because they don't want to share their jelly candy with you!

Work ethics seem to vary in college, and yet students highly voice their opinions aloud. The difficulty with preventing cyber-plagiarism on a superficial level is that you never get to the root of the problem, which is often just laziness. Students want a quick unchallenging way to write an essay that is due, because somehow they think that a lazy lifestyle in college will not catch up with them in the real world. ALL HABITS, good or bad, are going to follow you in the real world!! My second biggest regret about college was not developing a better work ethic. As an adult, I now see the consequences of wanting the "fast easy way" to life. The fast easy way to life leaves you with brief immediate gratification—but never leaves you with permanent joy. It is a sad, selfish lifestyle that will never challenge you to become anything greater than status quo.

Your goals do not decide your future; your habits do.

There is something just as important as a physical work ethic, and that is a *thinking* work ethic. Often people go to work, never thinking deeply—just to do their job, complain all day to coworkers, and then return home to watch television while eating their microwaved supper, passing by the dog dish while suddenly remembering that there is a reason the puppy is not happy. He is playing dead in the neighbour's backyard to make a political statement to the community about their abilities to raise pets!

Students often go to school, maybe wearing jogging pants or pajama bottoms disguised as pants, to drink their coffee, write a couple of notes, and hope that the professor will think for them and hand them a paper with all their questions answered. This would render them unable to problem-solve at any level of heightened creativity or cutting-edge innovation. They want to put their four years into the "grind" to be handed a degree. They want to be awarded a Ph.D without using their imagination or vitality, and be rewarded

with a fulfilling, high-paying job. They are working for the dental benefits instead of a challenge, only to find their careers unfruitful and stifling. An employee who gives up creative thought, simply to save effort, will become mindless. Lack of thinking is also laziness!

Intellectuals should never expect others to do their thinking and creative problem solving for them. That "somebody else can fix the problem"—should be you!! My pastor always says, "If it needs doing, do it!" College is a place where ideas and governmental policies can be discussed.

If ideas are what change the world,
then we need to have some.

In order to have ideas we must first be thinkers. We must subscribe to a policy of rational thinking, and amuse ourselves with investigation. We must be willing to challenge our own minds and hearts. We must be willing to analyse our own way of doing things, and constantly challenge ourselves to change. This always involves a *thinking* work ethic that must continue and grow past the graduation ceremony.

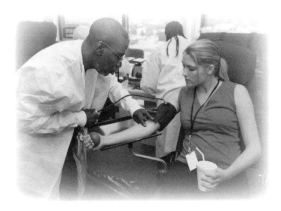

Many young people enjoy the concept of situational ethics, because it allows them to live for "the now". Living for the immediate pleasures of life allows them a quick rush of excitement. The sad reality is that often those closest to them end up paying for their "quick fix". Living for immediate gratification also clouds a person from seeing the rapidly advancing consequences. The consequences of poor ethics will not just be the loss of employment and loved ones. The consequence of situational ethics will be eternal loneliness. Selfish people rarely experience the joy of loving others, and the empowerment of maturing. The fast, easy way to life depletes your soul of depth and caring. **LOVE IS A VERB.**

"WE GET YOU": WORDS OF WISDOM

At my college, division was hard to maintain. Every ethnicity had their club. That's what I hated. If you're at college, you should be one big group, not separated. Segregation still does exist.

GREG FRY, BSc Political Science, **University of Maryland**

Sexual Harassment occurs when a hostile environment is created that interferes with a person's ability to do their work. Professors are there in the department to help students to do their work. A student should not have demands placed on them other than on the basis of their education, that would undermine students' "same opportunity" to an education.

ABIGAIL C. SAGUY
Ph.D, **Princeton University**
L'École des Hautes Études en Sciences Sociales: Paris

GETTING BAD MARKS IS <u>NOT</u> GROUNDS FOR "HARASSMENT" AGAINST YOUR PROFESSOR. If you have substantial concerns with marking discrepancies:

1) Keep records of ALL your papers in question.

2) Document the issues factually as they arise.

For example, if a Science major receives lower marks on their lab assignments than seems appropriate—submit written evidence (written assignments, course outline of expectations, and recorded, documented conversations with the professor or lab attendant) to the Dean. If there is valid proof and factual documentation that support your position, the inappropriate mark could be adjusted in your favour.

S. M., MSc Chemistry, **University of Saskatchewan**
BSc, **University of Regina**

Rape dates at parties; the date drug in the drinks, don't over-drink yourself so you're not aware of your surroundings.

MARYANN QUINN, M.Ed. Minor in reading, **University of St. Francis**

Our life is a reflection of our own choices. If our lives are not a success, it is because of our fears and beliefs, and not our circumstances that have held us back. Philosophy gives us the tools to see how those ideas that debilitate are illusions. Once we see what is false, we can use other disciplines give us tools to establish authentic habits.

DONALD HENDERSON, B.A. Philosophy, **Lakehead University**

I think at UCLA we are doing a nice job of education, and if assault victims do not want to come to us for help, they can go to a women's help center. IT IS O.K. TO REPORT AN ASSAULT. Obviously if we can prevent an assault, that is the best solution; however, girls need to know that we will help them if they need us to. That is what sets us over and above.

NANCY GREENSTEIN
M.S. Social Work, **UCLA**
Ph.D Eduction, **UCLA**

Don't go to frat parties. I went to one, and saw people getting drunk, and the girls getting taken advantage of.

TERESA LESTER; B.S. Elementary Ed. , **Franciscan University of Steubenville**

Students who are victimized are not often reporting crimes that have been against them, because they are scared to tell their parents the crime occurred while they were engaging in an activity that their parents would disapprove of. They would rather keep quiet, try to handle the situation in their own way, and spend the next 10 years struggling emotionally rather than just open up to their parents and get the help that they really need.

CAPTAIN MIKE PERRY, **East Carolina University,**
Campus Safety Division
B.S. Sociology, **Sul Ross State University of Texas**
M.S. Personnel Management, **Central Michigan University**

Students do not often come forward to report sexual harassment for fear of retribution from their harasser. Students however, in general, seem to be more knowledgeable about harassment now. When they see resultant action taken against harassers by an institution, they are more likely to formally report harassment incidents in the future. Students also find it easier to report harassment if they feel comfortable with the harassment officer or a faculty member that they can discuss the incident with.

As the sexual harassment officer for my college, I am required by law to take action and investigate the incident if a student comes to me describing the situation and provides the names of the alleged harassers. It is important for the student to know that if I am informed of the matter, I will be addressing it. This is why at our dental institution, we offer a two-hour class that informs students about what is or is not sexual harassment, what one should do if they are sexually harassed or see someone else being sexually harassed, and the process for reporting it. We have been very proactive at my institution regarding this issue.

KAREN P. WEST, D.M.D., M.P.H., Associate Dean for Academic Affairs,
University of Kentucky College of Dentistry
M.P.H., **University of South Carolina**
D.M.D., **University of Louisville, Kentucky**

You cannot develop morality at a university. It's about the individual. I had several classes in ethics, but fundamentally your ethics come from within, not externally. University teaches you nothing about owning a business; it's all technical. Even management tends to be post-graduation studies. It didn't teach me common sense. There's a lot of alcohol involved in becoming an accountant or in business, and schmoozing is a major part of getting clients. I have a few partners who are all good at business.

BILL BOGAR, B. Comm.
Commerce & Finance Accounting & General Business,
minor in Computer Science, **University of Saskatchewan**

I want to comment on your statement that students coming from functional homes facing pressures of college, negatively affects their ethics: (a response to an email)

I teach ethics, and find it very interesting how the students' opinions vary so much. First, we have to ask what is a "functional home"? Do we mean a normal environment? What is a normal family environment? Normal is a relative term. What is normal to one person is not normal to another. I find that in some homes domestic violence is normal. Alcoholism is normal—their families have been exposed to these two problems for many generations, and the students think this is normal. Is it normal? To whom is it normal? In my ethics class, we talk about many, many ethical issues throughout the 3 main components of criminal justice: law enforcement, corrections, and courts. I hand them scenarios and we have to discuss them. It is amazing how the opinions vary. I did my master's thesis on what people think is acceptable theft. Is it a pen from work? Is it a handful of grapes at the grocery store? Is it computer paper from work? Or maybe it's a dollar value. Is it $1 or $10? It's an ethical decision. And these decisions are derived from a variety of issues that have formed their ethical background and guided their decisions and behaviors.

If we discuss college issues, we are entering a whole different zone. The majority of my students are pretty ethical. But, I will run into a student that doesn't think cheating, or getting lab notes (even though they were absent) an ethical problem. Their main goal is to succeed. This drives many, many students. They will do whatever it takes to get the grade and pass the class. In ethics we have to separate and define which behavior is illegal (unlawful), and which behavior is just unethical—yet not illegal. I have found that through my survey on the thesis, the many years I have worked in the security field, or just teaching, everyone has a way of justifying their behavior. It might not seem rational to others, but they have a way of justifying what they did, and tend to dismiss the behavior. To others who are a bit more ethical, it seems very unethical, and find it difficult to believe what we hear and what their justifications are.

SUZANNE MONTIEL, Criminal Justice Instructor,
Nash Community College
A.A., **Santa Fe Community College**
B.S., **Fayetteville State University**
M.S., Law Enforcement and Loss Prevention, **North Carolina Central University**

I wish students knew how to come to work on time, and I wish they had a better work ethic. Generally kids just want things handed to them, because that was how they were treated in high school. A majority of high school students then enter the gates of college and are totally unprepared for the level of work they will have to do to succeed. The aggressive, hard-working achievers are becoming a minority these days.

JIM ROSS
M.S. Agriculture, Agricultural Biology Major,
B.S. Agriculture, Wildlife Science Major, **New Mexico State University**

ETHICS: "Your boss or profession may think it appropriate to hoodwink someone in order to get what you want in order to further your career. And while your name may be etched in gold somewhere at the end of your rise of popularity, all the people you stepped on to get to the top will vomit when they see it."

BILL CRAIG, Cum Laude B.A. Journalism, cum Laude BA. in English,
Mesa State College

Keep your mind open to new experiences. Experience all you can, but stay safe. In general, experience all you can when you're young, but you're naive then, so be careful. I would walk many blocks at night time; anytime someone could have gotten me. Try to learn something from each experience good or bad, large or small.

KAREN DAISY-SHIRIAEV, B.S. Therapeutic Recreation, **Indiana State University**

Pour your own drinks at a party; it just seems very unsafe right now, the way the media and the world throws things out their about people putting things in your drinks for jokes and date rape.

KATHY WYZOMIRSKI, Certificate in Health Administration,
University of Saskatchewan

Stop drinking. I didn't drink. My friends that often drank did not fare out as well.

SUSAN ZAHN, B.S. Accounting, **Indiana University**

you are not alone

Volunteer for acts of service in university. It sets the pattern for your life. Teach your daughters: you are the receiver in sexual relationships. The girl will be most vulnerable. The responsibility and consequences will lie on your shoulders. The woman has the body changes, shame, embarrassment, and diseases, more than the man. Go to the bathroom early in the morning before anyone else gets there. It's cleaner then. You're learning from so many different majors. Pick people's brains. You're exposed to so much information. After college, I realized that university is an awesome time to philosophize late at night. Expand your mind and horizons. Once you begin your career and family, there are less chances to just share ideas and learn.

CHEVAWN MUSUMANO, BSc Nursing, **Franciscan University of Steubenville**

Sexual assault on and off college and university campuses is still high. There continues to be a strong division between public and private life in the media, academic circles and everyday social practices. Sex, whether consensual or by assault is considered a private matter. Therefore, women feel very awkward in approaching the subject with strangers, who are often those positioned to help victimized women. It is a further problem that women are expected to "police men and male aggression". In other words, women are held accountable and blamed for enticing, luring and even seducing men into committing sexual assaults. In reporting the crime of sexual assault, it is woman's character that is under scrutiny. Police continue to mistakenly believe that women fabricate rape. This mistaken assumption, on the part of police officers, results in the re-victimization of assaulted women in an attempt to protect the "accused" men's good reputations. The presumption of innocence of men and guilt of women reflects the continued power imbalance resulting from unequal gender relations.

DR. VICTORIA BROMLEY, **Pauline Jewett Institute of Women's Studies/School of Canadian Studies**
Ph.D Political Science, **Carlton University**
M.A. Political Science, **York University**
B.A. History/ Political Science, **York University**

My parents often referred to the Bible passage that the wise man seeks the company of other wise men, but a fool finds his joy in other fools. It's not that you can't spend time with unbelievers, but you normalize things in your mind when it's all around you. We naturally acclimate to our surroundings. Where you find your council is the direction in which you are headed.

JULIE GHEEN, MBA, **Franciscan University of Steubenville**

From a Christian perspective I would have to say keep in touch with a minister from your church. STAY CONNECTED WITH HOME! When you attend college, even if it is a Christian college, there are different religious and ethical backgrounds entering the college. Professors will challenge your belief system because they want you to have your own faith, not your parents' faith. They will not give you solid answers after offering you information to think over, which is good—but at that age you are very impressionable. You need to know what you believe strongly and keep it.

DEIDRE BENNEWEIS, B.A. Organizational Communications,
Oral Roberts University

College did not teach me faith; my faith grew because of college. My experience was specific to Seminary. Seminary did not teach me things I thought it would. However, I grew in things of faith because of Seminary.

REV. LESLIE HAND, **College of Emmanuel and St. Chad**

If you are going to work in the hospital for a career, you must get used to the smell.

MYRNA MCDIARMID, BSc Home Economics

In the absence of care and compassion, competency and credentials have very little significance.

JANN BRADLY, R.N, N.P. **Montreal General College**

Often, the lie that is perpetuated is that knowing nothing about the evils of the world is equivalent to being innocent and pure, as God originally ordained us to be. Over and over, this lie has caused incalculable suffering to those who have had their innocence torn from them unwillingly, and consequently feel unclean and ashamed. As I continue to pray and talk with my Lord, I have become more and more convinced that purity is not the same as naivety or "blessed" ignorance. No, such ignorance about the evils that exist in the world around us is not only unrealistic in today's society, it is also potentially dangerous for the "innocent" involved. The naivety of a young person is easily taken advantage of in this world, and the consequences are often dire.

Proverbs 20:9 says, "Who can say, "I have kept my heart pure; I am clean and without sin"?" Instead, the purity of the heart and mind are not connected with ignorance, but rather with a real knowledge of the evils that exists around us, and a rejection of that evil. Purity is not a circumstance that is beyond our control as human beings, but rather a choice that every individual must make in his or her lifetime.

In closing, Philippians 4:8 encourages us to make a choice: "Finally, brothers, whatever is true, whatever is noble, whatever is right, whatever is pure, whatever is lovely, whatever is admirable—if anything is excellent or praiseworthy—think about such things." The author does not say, "remain ignorant to evil", but rather, "choose to think about that which is good before the eyes of God." And that, my friends, is something that every young person needs to know, that is not taught by university.

CHRISTINE, Political Science major, **University of British Columbia**

I enjoyed my college experience. Since I attended a Christian university, professors were very open to incorporating spirituality into academics in class and assignments. God and Science can co-exist! I wrote a compare/contrast paper on the Holy Spirit and Conscience. My professor appreciated it, in fact. My university taught me to be a well-rounded human with good ethics.

AYA F., B.A., B.Ed. AD, **Concordia University, College of Alberta**

TIDBITS FROM MOM:

Someone told me a long time ago that the definition of a rut is a long grave. So step out and do the things you never did in the past. When you are facing new challenges or fears, search for the possibilities, not the impossibilities.

Remember nothing is impossible with God. Watch and see God's miracle! Don't be afraid to live exited!

Remember: Faith does not always follow human advice.

Remember: Hugging is healthy and drastically improves our immune system with no side effects. Love and live to be a blessing to others.

CHERYL HENDERSON, R.N., **Confederation College of Applied Arts and Sciences**, N.P. Lic. Min., **W.I.B.I.**

CHAPTER EIGHT

College did not teach us how to be global citizens

"College is just a tool"

When I was a bubbly young girl, flittering around the house like a delicate butterfly, I often enjoyed listening to the soft humming of my mother's favourite church hymns. She baked fresh loaves of bread every week and prepared succulent peaches for canning every summer, that we had enthusiastically picked on our vacations to British Columbia. I watched her with admiration as she worked diligently to provide food on a limited budget for her three young children. While attending nursing school, my mother worked evenings in the emergency dept. answering phones, and would often cut hair on the weekends for grocery money. When we lacked groceries she grew a garden in our backyard, ensuring that her resourcefulness would protect us. Hardships during nursing school taught her the art of giving while surviving on a student's budget. Once she began working full time as a registered nurse, she continued to show charity to others in our impoverished neighbourhood—regardless of her financial circumstances.

My mother remembered what it felt like to walk in frigid –30° celsius Canadian winters with three children because we could not afford a car. As we took each step, she would always smile and have us sing along with her as though we were on an adventure that was unstoppable and exciting. Despite her cheerfulness, I knew it was freakin' cold—my feet felt numb after the first twenty minutes, but I didn't have the nerve to argue with her. I did not always sing each day, but she did. My mother was a woman full of hope, so passionate about life that she could offer mercy in a world full of cruelty.

I was always perplexed when she invited strangers over for lunch every Sunday after church. She would wake up early each Sunday morning and put a roast in the oven, making buns or pies before the morning sun welcomed her. She often looked disheveled at the service, but her servant's heart surrounded her like expensive jewels. After each church service, she would hug new faces and invite regular attenders as though it was the first time that they had ever dined with her. There were gentle elderly women from the church who lived alone that would accept my mother's invitation. My mother went out of her way to invite other struggling single moms who didn't know how they were going to feed their children that day. She would also have a loaf of bread hidden in the freezer to send home with them, when no one was watching.

The older couples would drink Earl Grey tea and tell amusing stories to the children who could not find a comfortable chair left. They would recount with delight the older days and how the community worked together, while the visiting children would play with my toys and listen from a distance. They were enjoying the fellowship around a meal cooked with unselfish love. My mother's hospitality warmed their hearts like the soft summer sun does on the sand. I often demanded with insistence in private, that my mother explain to me *WHY* she would offer our expensive pies and baked bread "to the world" when she worked so hard to make ends meet.

She always replied with the same softly whispered speech: "No one should be alone at Sunday dinner."

"Can they not eat at their own home?!" I often replied, while stomping my foot as though I were in sole custody of her well being.

She simply smiled and recited, "The Lord's mercies are new every morning... Paula, GREAT IS HIS FAITHFULNESS."

One morning my mother walked into our dilapidated townhouse after work, saying with tears in her eyes that the neighbours a couple of houses down had escaped a fire. The neighbor children had to watch their house burn to the ground all evening, while standing in the cold—dressed only in their pajamas while crying in shock and horror. Warm tears welled up in my mother's intense brown eyes, as she told us passionately to go to our rooms and collect some of our clothes and toys for those traumatized children.

Hesitantly, I walked up the stairs, feeling as though my legs were made of concrete. With each step, I gripped my green garbage bag with horrified angst to find things, *my* things, to give charitably and anonymously to these homeless children. Looking back, I know that

I was more distressed about giving them my newest toys, than the loss that they had suffered. I really loved all of the soft fuzzy sweaters that my loving grandmother knitted for me, and the exciting colorful toys that my father sent me on every holiday without fail.

Later that week after the fire, I was sitting impatiently on a cold school bus, trying desperately to see out the frosted window by scratching off the ice. The only thing that made the long tiresome ride towards my school interesting was watching all the new buildings being built in the downtown core. As a child, I loved watching the city grow and prosper—signaling lasting colourful change. The bus was sooo cold that morning that I had to clap my hands and stomp my feet. When it was well below zero outside, the school bus could not produce enough heat. I felt an unanticipated jerk as we came to an abrupt halt to pick up my neighbors' little girl who had lost their house. I was intrigued and mesmerized by the little aboriginal girl with shiny dark hair and beautiful charcoal eyes, with a warming smile that melted my heart in the unforgiving cold. I remembered seeing her play alone in the park, where my friends and I would keep to ourselves on the swing set.

I wish now that I had asked her to join us—showing her my kindness before the fire tragedy. I wished I had taken the time to meet this enchanting sweet young aboriginal girl that sat at the front of the bus so that she felt protected by the bus driver. I hadn't taken the time in the park to even ask her name. She looked different and acted shy, and I thought it would be too 'difficult' to have another friend over to the house—even though my mother *always* had extra yummy peanut butter cookies baked.

As this tiny girl slowly stepped onto the bus with hesitation, she tightly clasped one of the toys that I had anonymously given her. Her eyes were full of joy, as though the kindness from her neighbors held her heart lovingly and close like the hands of God would. That toy—*my tavourite toy*—was very important to her. After the fire, it was one of the few toys that she had. She took it everywhere, showing the toy to everyone all day long at school as a testament that she was *important* and her community loved her. She took the toy with her to school, demonstrating to the teachers that she was a young little vivacious girl who could and would survive heartache. It was that morning I realized what a beautiful woman my mother was. She was speaking the truth when she whispered "the Lord's mercies are new every morning". It was that frosty winter morning when I learned through the eyes of a child's innocence that it is truly better to give than to receive.

That chilly winter morning was when I realized that I wanted more from life than just a house, two kids and a Volvo. I discovered that I wanted to care about people who are left with nothing, using my future career in a way that blesses—not curses—my community. I suddenly felt motivated to feed people so that they do not have to eat alone. Now I want to take the time to meet other people "in the park", whether in my country or another, who are different and perhaps a little shy. We are becoming a global village with our technology, not our hearts. We want to learn about other cultures, but not necessarily share with them. It is human nature to be reserved instead of embracing others who are 'not like us'. The most important life-changing step a student can make is offering kindness to those who are 'different'.

My mother has become a successful nurse practitioner; yet her title is not what motivates her. She genuinely cares about her community, and wants to bless all of those people in the north she is neighbours with. They mean so much to her, and I often question if the people in her community value her acts of love. Of course they do—otherwise she would not be so happy in the far remote north of Canada. Perhaps jaded bureaucrats take for granted how much she helps the community in her care. The people she fed remember her kindness; sleeping under their warm quilts, cherishing the woman who taught them to sew. College will not teach you to become a caring humanitarian, nor will it turn you into a Nobel Peace prize-winning medical doctor. The daily personal choices you make, while studying and working, will define your character. Your ability to care starts with you.

Each choice you make will determine your destiny!

So many students become disillusioned by their second year of college, because perhaps they feel they are owed something. They tend to feel a sense of entitlement, after paying bills that equal the value of a starter home. The only thing you are owed from your four years of college is a degree, *if* your classes and GPA meet the graduation requirements. *The university does not owe you your soul.* If you offer your soul and all that you are to a group of self-absorbed intellects, leaving you jaded, you can only blame yourself. You can only blame yourself for 'selling your soul' and your creative thinking for such a small reward! If you have compromised and wrote a paper just to receive an 'A' rather than standing up for what you believe, then *you* are the one that decided that day to be a follower, not a leader. It was not the "system"—it was not the "little guy versus the big guy". It was you versus your conscience.

Survival Tip #21:

I pray daily that my destiny involves me sitting on the beach at St. Tropez all day watching cute French men walk by; however, in case you and I are called to do something else, we'd best not sit on the couch drinking lattés and practicing.

Intelligent students, who have been told all through high school what to think, are seeking desperately to experience four years of challenging thought and enlightenment at college. They just don't realize in their youthful ignorance that enlightenment takes more than earning a degree. Many students want the results of having new ideas and being challenged, but not necessarily the work that surrounds those benefits of study. Often students desire to be wise without making the effort to seek out the truth. It is much easier to relax and watch life occur than to engage in a life-altering volunteer effort.

Some students avoid volunteering because it takes time to care about others. Volunteering and travelling forces a person to see the world from a different view. These kinds of enriching experiences leave the learner as vulnerable as the people they have helped, because "looking good" is not enough. People who have not learned to look deeper than the "shell" of people and

communities are often disillusioned by the frailty they see in human beings. It is always easier to place more importance on how people look, than to love who they really are. College will not teach you to be bold and search for truth. You must be bold and search for truth yourself. People are like a book; they need to be lovingly opened and read to truly be understood.

University is merely an educational institution paid for by your tuition, government funding and possibly alumni sponsors, to train you in a specific field. What you do with that training is your decision. College courses are merely a tool designed to teach specific skills, to help you become a capable cog in your nation's economic wheel. Professionals are often reminded that they are a dime a dozen by society, but the best are not. The doctors who care about their patients and are driven to promote change, are valued. Doctors who donate their time to save children are not a dime a dozen. Where are you going to be in ten years? If all you have before your eyes is career advancement, than you need to ask yourself if you are self-absorbed. Sacrificing your community for status will leave everyone damaged. Everyone should make decisions that bless their community.

Look around; who helped you get to university? Who inspired you while you were there? Who cleaned the floors that you flippantly walked on with your muddy winter boots because you were in a hurry to get to your Algebra class? What is your Economics prof's first name? Did you pay attention to him or her, or were you more worried about their grading system? Each day you have an opportunity to 'think outside of yourself.' You have a chance to climb out of the box, and put it in the garbage permanently. If you do not practice this in four years of studying at university, I guarantee that you won't practice it in your career! It will be one very lonely career if that is the only path you are choosing to take

Learning philosophy in your freshman year will not help you find yourself.

In helping others, you will find yourself.

The university is a system, with walls, books and hallways. A university functions progressively when students attend classes, bringing with them a desire to learn and the self confidence to form new ideas. FEAR is the very reason that many young students are unable to define who they are and what their role is within this system. They don't know what they have to offer. They walk the hallways, never really knowing whether they are noticed. This suits a student who only finds college as a means to an end. They can go, hurry through their courses and then conquer life. Then there are aspiring intellects who want to attend classes, and want to know that their four years at college meant something. They want to begin their journey of life-learning.

For an adult student or international student who already values the journey of life-learning, this type of system can be daunting. Many adult students and international students want desperately to be challenged and earn a degree.

Since they have adult expectations placed on them, they are also bound by the fear of failure. Some of those students have children to support, debt to repay, and simply find it difficult to take a risk with next month's rent. This may be their last opportunity to begin something new, and they don't want to take too many risks. Many have already been in the work force; some are well travelled; and some have a varied educational background, already aware of what their defined roles and expectations are. The university, however, is NOT similar to the work force. University teaches students to research and analyze, not necessarily how to adapt to whichever system they are engaged in. For an adult or international student, university is a system within in a system, which is emotionally draining and difficult. It is challenging for someone with expectations to embark on the journey of life-learning, because there are no guarantees that the path they take will bring security.

Often those students who succeed are the ones who not only handle pressure, but use the pressure for their success. In the work world, it is much easier to be a creative individual than in the academic setting. Part of this is because professors are aspiring to achieve a specific ideology, and the students are conforming to a country's social majority as they are required to engage in many group projects and assignments. Individuality and independent thinking seems to be depleting as globalization is strengthening. I do not believe the loss of creative thought is simply due to globalization; perhaps there is just a dependency on technology. Students enjoy connecting globally online and through the media because the information is immediate. The facts are immediate, but learning how someone FEELS about the event takes time to understand. Understanding how a community was affected requires thinking about the impact it has on them and the world. Sometimes students want others to think for them because it is easier than attracting strife with others about social politics; they do not want to comprehend.

For most international and adult students, accepting others is part of realising that college communities are becoming global and it is important to embrace other cultures. In other words, it is very common now to see many international students and just as common to study overseas for a year or two while attending college and university. *"The world is becoming smaller".* Although some students and their parents are fearful of travel due to political unrest, the desire to embrace other cultures and languages is growing. In order to succeed now in the global marketplace, my generation is going to have to do business with other countries and other cultures. It is very difficult to have successful business meetings when the entrepreneurs involved are absolutely incapable of understanding their foreign business partners.

Seeking to understand is much easier than trying to be understood!

Some view acceptance of other nations as a loss of national independence, weakening a country's own national pride. However, the more international we are become, the more we learn that we are *interdependent* on each other. No country can be in a modern war without allies. Very few countries make goods that are only sold in their own nation. We are exporting goods and importing goods. That fact itself is making the work force global. Simply put, we are no longer selling bread and jam to just our neighbours. **We need other countries just as much as they need us.**

For this reason, it is important for students to learn at least the basic elements of other countries and their cultures. It is important to understand basic principles that different cultures live by. Even knowing some of the capital cities of other nations would make you look wiser. For example: the capital of Canada is OTTAWA, not Toronto! Canadians do not live in igloos; they hibernate in front of the television drinking coffee during hockey season... weeping as they watch our Stanley Cup go to some team that probably never grew up around snow. That's right; I bet some people don't even know what a "toque" is! We'll just have to get used to "being bullfrogs in a hailstorm" and be more prepared for next year!!

As an adult student I observed the evolution of teaching and learning. In the 80s when I attended high school, participation was valued and encouraged. It was very rare to see group projects and course evaluations. Written communication was the primary form of modern advancement that was integrated in the course curriculum. In the 90s, communication was only valued IF it conformed to the TEAM agenda, with the right level of emotions being asked for. Now, because of technological advancement and global thinking, students not only have to compete internationally to achieve high marks through memorization of facts, but are also expected to have well developed social skills, whenever they have group discussions which may now be virtual.

Although these new expectations sound whimsical to those of us that are older, survival in "the group" depends on it! Generation X has entered the work force with a loud, resounding boom. They have already proven, by the way they are treating older workers in the work force, to be young "cut-throats" who are willing to win at all costs. For today's student, college has become one big game of survival.

I would have much preferred as an adult student to avoid the added stress of competition by taking "external" university courses; however, that is a more recent development. These external degree classes would have been a more efficient use of my time! External degree courses offer older students more privacy and flexibility. The one-on-one experience with a professor helps those who need to build confidence with their written works. With the growth of the Internet, there is an increased variety of online college classes being offered. With the increasing growth of external degree programs, all adults who need to re-educate due to manufacturing plant closures will eventually study online or telecommute. Most adult students are studying because they have families to support, or forced to leave the field in which they are skilled.

In order to embrace the changes due to globalization, the universities are adapting to the new world market. As exports grow, careers are changing and evolving. For those experiencing these changes, transitioning from one specialization to another can be very difficult. Since I have graduated, I have received disdain from some interviewers who do not value my professional cooking background on my resumé. However, it is now said that it will be common for my generation to change careers at least three times before retiring. In today's rapid change, it is no longer "the norm" to stay in a specific field for forty years. My generation is also becoming more self-aware and confident in what they desire to do for the next ten years. Although some might view us as "transients", we are merely adapting to the demands of the global marketplace.

The reality universities are facing right now is that globalization has been a catalyst for permanent change in how we study. It's normal now for adult students and young people entering college to complete their first year online. It's now becoming feasible to study their entire four years online with a college from a different country. A student from a third world country can  take a four year degree online at a North American university. Let's just hope these countries don't create a hockey team out in the desert good enough to take *OUR* STANLEY! I really am trying to get my head around the fact that a Southern team took our Stanley Cup; but it makes as much sense as watching a Southern man get out of his truck to ask a woman for directions.

Completing a degree online has become a very popular movement, which has pros and cons. The benefit of doing college online is the personal ease that it offers. A student can learn on their own time, phone a professor and have their absolute attention (*if* you can reach them; some like to hide!), with four hours of learning that works around their schedule. The other 'pro' of learning online is the greater financial ease in which a student can study and still work at their current job. A student can now work full time in their country of origin, while completing a degree from another country. However, as discussed in the cyber world chapter, there is a loss of experienced synergy and personal human touch.

Synergy has a very powerful effect on individuals. It is the interaction with other classmates that sharpens your mind and sparks philosophical debate. Both approaches to college are equally advantageous. There is value to the social interaction with other students and experiences outside of the insular thinking that young people often have.

Survival Tip #22:

Buy a good college-level dictionary so that you can understand what on earth the debate is about in your International Relations class. Apparently, telling your classmates that free trade was a good idea because they opened a new coffee stand on campus, is not actually all that impressive to them!

One reality holds true in the college sphere that will not be eradicated... globalization is no longer a concept, and technology has ushered in the new global culture with a roar. Technology is here to stay! It is said that text messaging will even be replacing emails in the next year. The social and educational dynamics have changed in society and in colleges; we will never be reverting back to "the way college was done" in the 60s. A student who wants to embrace globalization is going to have to "ride the technology train"—advancing with technology, even though they have still not taught their mothers how to "text message" in cryptic short form!

Telecommuting *(no, that does not mean getting up and bringing the phone to your good-looking brother repeatedly because college girls keep calling the house to flirt with him)* has become a favourable solution for the workforce seeking to advance in the midst of globalization. Telecommuting is also becoming a solution for adults who have been forced to re-educate due to corporate downsizing and organizational restructuring. Not only does my generation have to re-educate and discover new talents—we must compete at an international level. For American telecommuters, this may not be as challenging as it is for older Canadians who are pioneering the modern service industry.

If young students are not proactive, they may feel threatened by the demands of global competition. That is why it would be a great idea for a young person to travel. Travelling abroad, if it is affordable, helps a student learn to communicate in another language and learn the value of understanding a nation's heart and soul. The students who are going to succeed in the middle of globalization are the ones who know how to communicate effectively and bridge other cultures smoothly. It's a very difficult skill that can only be acquired by students who want to do more than just climb a corporate ladder. Travelling abroad enables a student to learn the art of communicating with other cultures rather than looking at pictures on the Internet. Although it would seem idealistic, travelling abroad is actually easier than one would think.

> *To accept other cultures with ease, there must be understanding and appreciation for them.*

The first step to travelling abroad is checking into it. All campuses have an abroad studies program with faculty who are very willing to help students travel affordably. It is very easy now to find the abroad program, because it is posted on the college or university website. There is also a very cutting-edge and dynamic magazine with all kinds of information and tips to help you live, work and study abroad: www.transitionsabroad.com. This magazine was founded by a proactive senior in university, who wanted to share international traveling and studying experiences. Often students feel that traveling is unattainable because they have never heard someone tell them how to do it. Here is the solution: ASK!

It is also a good idea to save for a trip abroad while you are still in high school if you know that you want to learn about another culture in order to enrich your education and chances for a dynamic career. Some of the ways that a high school student can begin saving is through fundraising,

you are not alone

scholarships, and through cutting costs while going to college (for example: spending their first year of studies living with their parents). Some students have even had an international experience by joining an international organization or teaching in a country that is desperate for English teachers. Not all international colleges are more expensive than your own. Join a goodwill trip that is in need of support staff, and they may be willing to pay for your plane ticket. If not, they may be experienced fundraisers and able to show you how to travel on a tight budget! Involve yourself in a small trip to learn the do's and don'ts of travel, before going somewhere drastically different from your own country. Ask some of your friends to accompany you on a small regional road trip during the holidays. Make a point of visiting a museum or historical site to learn more about the cultural background.

> ### The biggest expense with traveling to overcome is ignorance.

One really great cost-effective way to gain a global understanding or to have a good 'international experience' is to organize one at your school. If you feel that your school is culturally illiterate, then take some initiative! Host a club that attracts international students or join one that they might have already set up. Some international students would love to share with you what they eat in their country. Some of my greatest memories in college included the time I went to an African party which was very lively and alcohol-free, eating curried peanut chicken for the first time. I also heard them sing and had no idea how uplifting and exciting their music is. I laughed boisterously for hours.

I had equally as much fun at Asian parties, eating spring rolls and Malaysian chicken (who am I kidding, I have a weight problem causing my tummy to look like a teddy bear... I hit whatever international party I could!) Why not spend Friday nights eating exciting new food for little cost and an enjoyable social atmosphere? It's too easy to fall into the "dirty tourist" trap, as they say in the international community. That is where students visit a nation for five days at a resort, and assume that because they ate resort food and read the local newspaper that they've had a "cultural experience" and are now familiar with the nation's politics and contemporary issues. Staying at a resort while on vacation will not allow you to see the delicate social elements of a region. A tourist travelling to Las Vegas for one week does not suddenly comprehend the United States and all of its foreign policy. Understanding how Americans think and act, takes time living with them and valuing their heritage. Appreciating the U.S. takes more than driving down Interstate 95.

As I was learning the Spanish language, I tried very hard to and still do keep in touch with the Spanish community. They are some of the most intoxicating people you will encounter. I have listened to some of the most fascinating stories as they warmed my stomach with *paella*, and charmed my ears with enchanting music. The Spanish people are cultured artists who value their communities, and love the laughter of children. Understanding how the Spanish people think and act takes time, sitting at their dinner table enjoying their natural hospitality and listening to their heart. To love the Spanish soul, you must first be intoxicated by who they are. There is not a book that can teach you how to linger over Tapas. Enjoyment of a culture comes from truly experiencing another human being, taking the time to value them. I developed a greater appreciation for their ability to tango, now that I've ended up in the emergency room receiving four stitches.

Hint: *If you are from the prairies and wear jeans, dusty cowboy boots, with a big ol' silver and gold belt buckle... you might not be ready for the tango! Try stepping to the beat first without getting hair in your eyes.*

Since my best friend is French, I had the wonderful opportunity to learn the nuances that only the French have. I did not realise that it is easier to just talk louder than the television, rather than turn it down! Without the help of my French roommate, I would never have learned that the world needs to decorate in pink and blue more often. I also felt very much "out of the loop" when I saw her family wave their hands dramatically as they spoke. Fortunately, I grew up in an Italian neighbourhood and understood angry voice reflections, trying to avoid conflict as I purchased grapes. During many of my college weekends, I tried earnestly to discover why most French people would think molasses on a plate with some toast is delightful. Hmmm... I am still confused about that one! However, myself being half-Ukrainian, I was unable to convince my roommate that cabbage rolls have nutritional value other than the FIBER they seem to offer.

There is a joy that comes from seeking to understand others and delighting in their differences. The process offers color to an ordinary canvas. Even though the international community is interdependent in the face of globalization, our individuality can be cherished. To achieve peace, international relations must be based on respect for the frailty of humanity.

In having respect for others, there must be a cooperation between sovereign states, reaching for practical and valuable solutions to common problems. This is the reason for treaties. The purpose of peace is to adopt a harmonious equilibrium for our international society.

If we are incapable at the college level of simply smiling at an international student or going one step further and introducing ourselves, how are we going to treat them when they are the CEO of an international company in twenty years? Take the initiative to include international students in your everyday activities. Since soccer is a universal sport, why not invite them out to a soccer game once a month? Sports often act as an ice breaker for students struggling with language barriers. After the game, take them out for dinner with a group of friends and have fun. International students are human beings that like to laugh as much as you do!

How you treat international people at college is how you are going to treat their country when you are in a position of power. You may not agree with every ideology that they have, nor do you need to. You simply need to learn the art of respecting others. Life-learners are willing to make an effort to understand people around them; willing to overlook differences and share what they have to offer. Even if you do not hold political office that influences another country, you will have neighbours, and you will have a vote. Your vote at the polls on election day will always have more power in a democratic nation than your job title ever will. What you acquire on your journey of life-learning will drastically alter your political indifference. When you care about those who are different than you, you suddenly learn to value what you have. People value the ability to vote when they see what others have been denied.

Determining to have a global mindset takes a conscious effort to communicate with others. The ability to exchange ideas is very important, in order to move between different cultures with ease. A student will only learn how to communicate effectively by risking new discoveries about other people. Rich geographical history and sophisticated culture are intertwined within people groups of any nation.

To grasp the political thoughts and present conflicts, a student must understand the geography and history of the nation in question. They must understand the steps that were taken to arrive at where they are.

They must learn about the nuances of other people to comprehend why they have retreated from negotiations. Fear and ignorance is only overcome by education and understanding.

This kind of education is only pursued by students who take initiative; by students who care more about others than financial success. You can only understand the world by first being part of it. Students have a choice; they can go to college and be status quo—only worrying about grades and money; or they can go to college and experience four years that matter. Four years that matter takes much more than spending money. Four years that matter takes much more than good studying skills.

To experience four years that matter at college, you will be required to care about something and someone other than you.

"WE GET YOU": WORDS OF WISDOM

As the world is becoming a smaller place through technology and travel, it is becoming more necessary than before to learn other languages for employment purposes in the future. Employment is becoming more international, and how you carry yourselves in foreign countries as an ambassador of your nation is crucial. We will rid ourselves of the 'dirty tourist' syndrome when we travel abroad by learning about other cultures with sincerity. To become deeper cultural learners is our responsibility as global citizens.

KRISTIAN CHERVENOCK, B.A. International Relations,
M.S. Higher Education, **Western Washington University**

I wish that students would come to university with a better education and understanding of World Matters; with a higher understanding in Christian world views. They do not seem to understand and know about the rich legacy of the Christian intellects that have gone before them. When Christian students often attend a secular college they are eaten up by the academic training, because they are not trained and prepared for debating, defending their beliefs and world views, and they are limited in their abilities to reason.

JEFFREY C. TUOMALA, Associate Dean for Academic Affairs,
Liberty University, Professor of Law
LL.M., highest honors, **George Washington University National Law Center**, Washington, D.C.
Postgraduate studies, **Ashland Theological Seminary**
J.D., **Capital University Law and Graduate Center**
B.S. Education, **The Ohio State University**

Do internships, if it's required or not in your study—employers aren't looking just for your degree, they're looking for experience and hands-on activities. Volunteer. Try new things, anything that interests you, because you never know if you'll like something if you don't try it.

MICHELLE BROOK, B.S.W. Social Work, **Cornerstone University**

Find a wise person, and park yourself at their doorstep. My French professor was my biggest influence, not just in knowledge, but wisdom and a zest for life. Don't lose your love of learning. Find a way to foster a positive attitude, so you squeeze everything you can out of 4 years of education. You may never have that opportunity again.

LESLIE GENUIS, B.A. French, Theology, Minor in English,
Franciscan University of Steubenville
B. Ed. French Immersion, **University of Regina**

There's more to life than Playstation. (and I don't mean X-Box either!)

NATHAN STANT, B.A. Education, **University of St. Francis**

The world that students today are facing is so much different from the world that I grew up in that it's hard for me to give advice. I think most of us fall into careers that we never expect, live in places we never thought we'd live, and that it's better to constantly reassess options and changing conditions than to have a hard-and-fast "five year plan." At least that's my philosophy. Things are always going to change—things will probably get better when you're at your lowest points, and things will never be as ideal as your dreams. I do think that students should try to realistically assess the probabilities of getting jobs related to their majors. There's a lot to be said for a broad liberal arts education, but I don't think that students should be encouraged to spend years in graduate education in areas where the job market is bleak.

MARY JO SCHNEIDER, Associate Professor (Anthropology),
University of Arkansas
Ph.D, **University of Missouri**

Even though you will attain extensive education, you may not utilize all the information you have received in university. Therefore, effective training is personal training. You will have a more effective training from involving yourself in activities, volunteering, and being very selective about the summer job that you have.

RENEE THIBAULT, former Commerce student

Try at least once: living in a dorm, coffee, playing a sport, going to church, and studying a lot!

MICHELLE SHANNON, M.P.T. Physical Therapy, **University of Michigan**

My biggest regret was not going to travel and study abroad. All of my friends did it, and they loved it and learned so much rich history. Once you get a job and start working, you have greater responsibilities and cannot just leave for four months. Two weeks during the summer is just not enough time to research the history of a Dutch city that is 2000 years old. Take a semester in a country abroad; it is such a great experience.

LISA NAGELMAKERS, B.A. Communications, **Wilfred Laurier University**

When I was young and going to high school at the public school (our reserve was very small, and our understanding of the world was small), I did not realize that my colleagues had a head start. We never talked about our future on the First Nations reserve; we only talked about 'getting a good job' and not which job. I wish someone had recognized that we needed good mentors and good councilors. Good mentors are key for the success of Aboriginal students who come from a reserve where community interaction is very important to them. Aboriginal people are very community-oriented, and need interaction with people they are close with. They need help in knowing what is a good fit for them, for college is not just a different world, it is a different lifestyle with many demands that will be placed on them. They also need help in discovering the larger world that they are a part of and how they fit.

DR. DEBORAH PACE
Ph.D Clinical Psychology, **Utah State University**
M.S. Psychology, **Utah State University**
B.A. Education, **University of Alberta**

Give more than you take. Every issue in your life; if you gave more than you took, there'd be no issue.

SANDY YOUNGHANS, B.S. Elementary Education

I wish that the students entering university and college would not be afraid to try new things. A student may come from a small town that does not have a museum, and be afraid of or unaware that there is a museum on campus full of fascinating artifacts. Our art museum also hosts international artist and academics. Students need to take advantage of all these cultural opportunities offered to them at college. Most international students who are well-traveled seem to treat culture like it is home for them. They do not enter a campus museum like it is a stoic church. My advice to freshmen is to realize the value of what they can learn culturally and how it will better position you for your encounter with the global community when you enter your career.

WENDY BREDEHOFT, Curator of Education
B.S.A, **University of Wyoming**
M.S.A. Visual Arts, **Vermont College**

You are almost certain to suffer some kind of academic disaster at some point. It may be a midterm you weren't prepared for, a group project with terrible partners or an essay that completely missed the mark. It may even be something that's completely outside your control. Being a successful student is not about never having failures. Being successful is about how you choose to react. And that is under your control. After a failure, some people give up inside—deep down they start to believe they can't do any better and it gradually becomes the truth. Other people get stubborn, dig in, and resolve never to be shaken. Confidence that you still have potential for success can keep you motivated for the hard work ahead. And hard work with motivation will bring you the success.

NICK, BSc Physics, MSc Computer Science

It's not what you teach children; it's what you learn from the children: Life experience, patience, and managing people. There's one employee who has very strong B.O. (body odor). He's a good worker, well groomed, but he stinks. How do you teach managers to deal with that? University didn't teach me that!

OLIVER, M.S. Microbiology and Anatomy/Physiology,
University of Hamburg, Germany

But as we all know, life is short. I can never retrieve the time I squandered—time I could have spent KNOWING my friends better, learning my lessons more precisely, faithfully keeping my commitments. I can only look back on the few, precious times I did let go of the troubles surrounding me, the times I let God work through me. I can look back on the time I got up at the crack of dawn to protest at the abortion clinic; the time I stayed up late to talk with and comfort a friend in my dorm; and the time I poured my heart and soul into my thesis; the week I spent my spring break in the Bronx, helping those less fortunate than myself. Over three years after graduating Franciscan, I know absence makes the heart grow fonder. I couldn't see what I was missing while I was there, I can only see what I could have had now that I'm gone. But God lives in the present, not in the past, with its trouble and regrets. His name is not I WAS, His name is I AM. Life after college has taught me to treasure what is in my life now, and as I continue to heal, and mature in my faith, I know that I am His, and every moment I have left in this world, I will be learning to live for Him.

ERIN JESSICA LYONS-SCHMITT, B. English **(Oxford, NJ)**, **Franciscan University of Steubenville**

Inspiration also comes from you learning what you like to do. You can want something, and it is a lot different from knowing you want something. You cannot know absolutely whether you will like what you are doing until you are doing it. However, university is not the place to guess at what you like. The university does not want you to guess at what you like either. A cheap way to learn your passions is to volunteer. University is not going to hand you your life.

YVONNE HENDERSON, former University of Carlton engineering student; College Diploma Web Design

Get involved and stay involved. Rely on your R.A. College isn't always about drinking.

DEANNA JAY, B.A. Family and Child Services, **Ball State University**

The world is becoming smaller just because of our international students that come to study. If you cannot afford to study abroad, make an effort to visit with the international students on campus. Make the first contact in an overt fashion since they are the ones that are new to your country. Usually, international students do not have a car, so why not invite one of them to go to Wal-Mart with you? They might really like the shopping experience. Traveling will show you the geography of a nation, not necessarily the heart of a nation. When you visit with someone, you learn about the heart and soul of their nation. Tourists only get to see a resort; they do not get to see the soul.

GLENNA A. DOD, D. Abbott Turner Professor of Free Enterprise and Division Chair of Social and Behavioral Sciences,
Wesleyan College, Georgia
B.S. **Eastern Kentucky University**
M.A., **Eastern Kentucky University**
Ed. D., **University of Southern Mississippi**

The primary reason it is important to study abroad or take trips in college to other countries is the job market and employers within the government sector and business sector are looking to hire students with a 'Global understanding'. Unless the student has an 'international experience', they will not understand the 'global phenomenon'. Students need a background in history, geography and languages to help them understand cultures and how they developed the political identity that they have. The best way for a student to maximize their traveling experience is to already have taken courses that aid in the learning process of the trip. A student will not enter the professional world and be able to understand contemporary issues and contemporary conflicts unless they can first put them in geographical and historical context.

DR. KENNETH HOLLAND, Professor of Political Science,
Kansas State University
B.A. Political Science, **Furnan University**
M.A. Political Science, **University of Virginia**
Ph.D Political Science, **University of Chicago**

I am very much in favor of being proactive! There are many ways to have an international education that is just as intense as an international experience. Join some of the international clubs even though you are not from that nation for the year. If you are trying to learn another language in college cheaply, post an add saying that you are willing to give free English lessons to international students willing to teach you their language. Then have coffee together once a week speaking only the other person's language. It is a real situation, rather than learning theory. You will experience how they experience life, not just learn a new language.

SHERRY SCHWARZ, Editor & Publisher, *Transitions Abroad* magazine
B.A. English, **Middlebury College, Vermont**

Enjoy life; don't let life enjoy you.

MARTIN ATARAMA, B.A. Physical Education, **University of Chiclayo, Peru**

Frankly, no one is ready for globalization; it is a game. It is a game that we are all going to play in the 21st century. Globalization is a culture where normative rules are changing. It is partly a response to the global ideas, the global market, the global economy and new global identity. People are not the same as they were 100 years ago, and we will never be able to be the same. Ideally, one would be able to move smoothly amongst the different cultures and peoples without receiving judgment for doing so. This is a very difficult yet profound skill to acquire.

DUANE W. CHAMPAGNE, Professor, Comparative/
Historical Sociology, **UCLA**
Ph.D Sociology, **Harvard University**
M.S. Sociology, **University Of North Dakota**
B.A. Mathematics, **University Of North Dakota**